Pubs o' the South

A Collection of Paintings and Drawings of the Public Houses of
Otago, Dunedin, Central Otago, Southland & Invercargill

John Husband

Published by Craig Printing Company Limited
PO Box 99, Invercargill 9840, New Zealand

© 2007 John Husband

ISBN 978-0-908629-66-4

Printed by Craig Printing Company Limited,
122 Yarrow Street, PO Box 99, Invercargill 9840, New Zealand.
Email: sales@craigprint.co.nz   Website: www.craigprint.co.nz

Foreword

Today, the social hubs of our communities are likely to be a mall, a supermarket, a multiplex or a stadium. When we think of hotels we see bland multi-national décor, suits, smart card room keys, broadband internet, satellite TV, mini-bars and dinky little shampoos.

John Husband gives us images, histories and stories of a different time when the pub was a pivotal, noisy, witty, and vital part of every large and tiny community in Otago and Southland (and mercifully still is in many of our southern country towns).

With or without my friend of 50 years (we've had a few together), I love going into pubs like the White Horse at Becks or the Vulcan at St Bathans and immediately feeling the locality and its history wrap around me. I love what John has done in this book too, blending his formidable art, research and his great "ear" for local yarns and colourful people.

Southern New Zealand needed this book and I can't think of anyone better to produce it. John Husband has painted, sketched, had a tincture or three, chatted, made music, talked, listened, or argued in or around every pub in our region. He came from some odd place up north but he's a southern man like few others.

John has given us a lot of good radio, jazz, art and journalism over the years; as its director for over 20 years, he's done more than anyone to create at Anderson Park the best provincial art gallery in the country; he's been Southland's visual archivist for decades and now in this book he has gifted our region with a wonderful record of our oldest and liveliest community assets . . . our pubs.

Good health and a kind wish, FJH.

Michael Deaker
Dunedin

Contents

Otago

Careys Bay Hotel................................6
Portobello...7
Chick's Hotel.....................................8
Strath Taieri 10
The Criterion 11
The Birthplace of a
    Motor Empire.......................... 12
Hotel South Otago......................... 14
Duntroon 15
Palmerston South 16
The Outram Hotel 17
The Catlins Inn, Owaka................. 18

Dunedin

The Bowling Green 19
The "Glue Pot" 20
The Mornington Hotel................... 21
The Crown Hotel 22
The Rugby....................................... 23
The Law Courts 25
The Royal Albert 26
St Kilda Hotel................................ 27
The Fitzroy..................................... 28
The Clarendon................................ 29
Prince of Wales 30
The Empire 31
The Waterloo.................................. 32
The Parkside at Caversham............ 33

Central Otago

The White Horse at Becks 35
"Vulcan, the God of Fire . . ." 36
The Lauder Tavern......................... 38
Cape Broome.................................. 39
Parts of Old Queenstown Survive . 41
John Marsh's Hotel, Cromwell 42
Rae's Junction 44
Memories of Coaching Days 45
A Victim of the Clyde Dam 46
The Original Royal 47
The Present Royal 48
History Side by Side, Lee Stream . 49
Stanley's Hotel, Macraes Flat........ 50
The Victoria 52
One of the First to Disappear 53
Maniototo, Art Deco..................... 54
Commercial Hotel, Omakau 57
Black's Hotel 58
The Stables, Matakanui.................. 59
Newtown Tavern, Matakanui....... 60
The Ancient Briton, Naseby 62
Wicked Willy.................................. 64
Shingle Creek 66
Chatto Creek 68
The Albion at Luggate 69
Eichardt's Hotel 70
Roxburgh's Commercial 72
The Royal Oak, Arrowtown 74
Welcome Home Inn, Skippers 76

Beaumont Hotel............................. 77
Clark's Junction............................. 78
Dansey's Pass Hotel 79
Buckham's Brewery 80
Bannockburn 81
Shotover Ferry Bridge Hotel 82
The White Star 83
Dunstan Hotel 84
Cardrona 85
The Railway Hotel at Ida Valley .. 87
Oturehua Tavern 88
Post Office, Chatto Creek.............. 89
The Pub at Poolburn 90

Southland

The Kingston Connection 92
Riversdale's Local 93
The Shamrock at Fairfax 95
Taylor's Creek Hotel 96
The Criterion at Round Hill 98
Commercial Tavern, Wairio.......... 99
The Hokonui Distiller................... 101
Thornbury Tavern 102
Mine Hostess – Peg Taylor........... 103
Lumsden's Royal Mail Hotel....... 105
Parawa Junction 106
All Alone at Benmore 109
The Garston Hotel........................ 110
Chub's Bar in Winton 111
The Waiau Tavern 112

The Royal, Waikaka...................... 113
The Winton Hotel 114
The Commercial, Mossburn 116
The Aparima Hotel....................... 119
Orepuki.. 120
Fifty-one Dry Years...................... 121
The Railway Hotel at Mandeville. 122
Harliwich's Carrington Hotel..... 123
The Green Roofs at Wallacetown. 124
Lorneville Junction Hotel 125
Colac Bay Tavern 127
The Pavilion 128
The Celtic at Browns.................... 129
The Club at Bluff......................... 130
The Bayview at Bluff.................... 131
The Railway at Nightcaps........... 132
Holland's Gore Hotel................. 133
The South Seas, Stewart Island .. 134

Invercargill

Waikiwi Bush Hotel 135
The Governor Grey 136
"The Ugliest Tavern Ever" 138
A Grand Old Lady........................ 139
The Cecil 140
Edwardian and Baroque Revival.. 142
Princess Hotel 143

The Royal Standard
    of England 144

Prologue

When I began drawing and recording the history of the buildings and people of the south I was advised by a wise old journalist that if I had arrived in an unfamiliar region, I must first go to the local pub, then to the cemetery. By then I would have the basis of the information needed to describe my drawings. How right he was . . . In the south of the South Island we appear to have our fair share of old hotels, particularly in areas that were first settled by those optimistic souls who were lured by the gold they believed lay just below the surface of the land and the river. Up sprang settlements with names such as Weatherstone, Muddy Creek, Kilkenny Hill, St Bathans, Vinegar Hill, Gabriel's Gully and Matakanui to name but a few of the quirky and sometimes exotic locations. Sadly, most of the mining camps were exotic in name only, but most of them had hotels! Previously uninhabited areas suddenly had up to 20 hotels lining the narrow winding main streets that formed the basis of towns like Lawrence and Arrowtown.

Thankfully some of these hotels have survived, despite being built of the materials of the land – sundried brick, wattle and daub and stone and schist. In this book I haven't attempted to record the complete history of all the many pubs I have known and loved or of all the publicans down through the ages, but more of my personal encounters with the hotels, their bars, their patrons, owners and staff. My recollections cover 54 years of wandering around this hugely diverse part of New Zealand, soaking up the history and the uniqueness of Southern New Zealand . . .

I doubt if there are many among us that, at some time in their life, haven't called in on a country hotel. We in Southland and Otago still have our share of "Classic Watering Holes". In the mid 1980s, entire rural settlements ceased to function simply because a political philosophy of the day decreed, that centralisation was "For the good of the country!" One commentator of the time remarked that "It may be good for the economy but it did bugger all for the individual rural town dweller" . . . how true.

What it did was to rip the heart out of hitherto flourishing service centres. First to go were the post offices, closely followed by the grocery shops, the bank branches and more recently the garage and its petrol pumps. The rail link had long gone as had the local bobby and his station, but some of the buildings remain and have been put to good use by the surviving communities.

When I came to Southland in 1956 there seemed to be a dairy factory on every rural corner. Often, the services clustered around these factories and completed the many villages that dotted our landscape, but remarkably, if the district had been blessed with a pub since its pioneer days, it was generally the only building that has survived.

It's quite ironic that in those far off days when these settlements were established, the first two buildings to be completed were the church and the hotel. Unlike today, these early hotels served the community and the traveller as a place to rest overnight and partake of the plain hearty meals of yesteryear. Nowadays the emphasis has shifted.

Today you can do a complete circuit of Central Otago by car in a day but when these hotels were first established, they were but a day's walk apart. What does it say about us when a hotel built in the 19th century is still refreshing the traveller, but the church built at the same time is full of hay bales, or has been converted to a dwelling for a modern day "lifestyler" . . . To further philosophise, I remember when I was growing up in the '30s, members of my family (except my father) wouldn't be seen dead in a town hotel, but considered a little hotel in the country quite acceptable.

I never comprehended that example of adult logic but I did enjoy the glass of raspberry flavoured lemonade as I waited in the back seat of the car outside. During this same era of my life, a couple of members of my family were country publicans in small towns and villages in the North Island.

In the late 1930s, an uncle slated the thirst of the locals and the weary traveller at lower Norsewood and later at Onga Onga in the Hawke's Bay. I can still see the mighty oak barrel sitting up at the end of the bar with its wooden tap protruding and sometimes dripping into the tray below. No sophisticated pressure system in those days. But it didn't deter the thirsty patrons. Later in his hotel life he moved to quite a grand establishment in a larger town in southern Hawke's Bay which boasted 56 bedrooms complete with balcony overlooking the main street and a magnificent dining room of which my aunt was very proud. Starched white tablecloths, monogrammed silver cutlery and crockery were set off by the polished wood panelling and ornate plaster ceiling. The main entrance to the hotel was on a grand scale too. Spacious, with an imposing tiled floor leading to a classic reception desk behind which rose the staircase. In my mind's eye now it resembled an old Hollywood movie set. When I stayed with my aunt and uncle I slept in one of those many bedrooms and a lasting memory is of the wash stand and its Royal Doulton wash bowl, jug and chamber pot. When this hotel was "tavernised" all of these toilet sets (more than 50 of them) were sent to the tip! Today you would have to raise a loan from the World Bank to afford to buy these now, much prized, treasures. Holidaying with aunt and uncle in a palace-like hotel was a great adventure for an impressionable child all those years ago.

Also in this book I will attempt to retrace my sometimes wobbly steps around Dunedin and its many pubs . . . In 1951, after a riotous ten day holiday at the Portage in Marlborough Sounds, I was persuaded by a bloke from Wellington that I should go home to Pahiatua, pack my belongings and join him and his flatmates in Dunedin where they were studying at Otago University. "Who knows," they said, "You just may tidy up your intellect". . . The search for knowledge was shortlived but my five years in "student town" were the best I had experienced in my short life. Yes, I did learn a lot, but only a small percentage of the learning was academic.

I managed to get my first painting *(Lawyer's Head)* hung in a dealer gallery and I was introduced to the Dunedin jazz scene – a scene I have been part of for the past 53 years. But my initiation into the art of after-hours drinking in the simply wonderful array of hotels in this Scottish city called Dunedin, played a large part in my adult development. More of that later in the book.

The year I arrived in Dunedin I was taken on a Central Otago tour of hotels. It began on the pretext that we would gather cheap fruit for the flat as money was always short, but of course, the only money spent was on petrol and Speights. From that day on I was sure that if I was to follow my dream of painting pictures and playing music, this was the perfect place to live and work. Southland and Otago have been kind to me and I thank everyone and everything that have enabled me to live my dream.

John Husband
Riverton

Carey's Bay Hotel

Henry Dench built this hotel in the mid-1870s after finishing Chick's Hotel in Port Chalmers . . . Carey's Bay was named after David Carey who came to Waikouaiti in 1840 at the suggestion of the legendary Johnny Jones. About 1848 the Careys and their five children moved to Port Chalmers where David was engaged in sawing, lime burning, brewing and lightering. He piloted the first vessel up the harbour illegally, as he was unlicensed. The family moved to what was to become Carey's Bay and in 1858 they were apparently the only residents. He went on to build the Blueskin Hotel, at the foot of "The Kilmog" in 1864 and ran it with two of his sons, David and Stephen. This hotel has been extensively restored by the present owners, Barry Colman and his late wife Cushla Martini. They flew down to Dunedin in 2001 for the Bledisloe Cup game at Carisbrook. We lost the cup and the day after, this couple from Auckland, drove to Port Chalmers and finished up buying this hotel. In 1982 local artist Ralph Hotere painted *Vive Aramoana* which is now in a Barry Colman's collection. This painting was painted as a protest against the proposed Aramoana Aluminium Smelter and it now hangs along with about 15 other Hotere works from local collections, on the walls of this beautifully restored hotel.

Portobello

The licence to trade as an hotel was granted to Nicholas Coneys on 22 April 1874. In the 1860s another hotel on a different site traded for a while but closed soon after this hotel was built. It has had a number of licensees over the years, among them three women. In 1882 Johanna Docherty dispensed good cheer and hospitality until 1901 when Eliza Nelson took the reins. Then followed William Allpress in 1945. In 1951 when I first visited this pub, after finishing a drawing in the rain, Evelyn McAuley was in charge until 1983 when Ernie and Faye Webster took over. This couple are still running this popular Otago "watering hole" in this most picturesque setting on Otago's Peninsula. More and more people are choosing to live on the hills above the bay – many of them commuting to their work in the city each day.

Chick's Hotel

Fred La Hood was one of Joseph La Hood's sons who made a sizeable contribution to commerce and the professions in early Dunedin. At one time he was the licensee of this legendary hotel at Port Chalmers. Chick's Hotel, according to the historic places plaque on this stone building, was built in 1876 for George and Ellen Chick by Henry Dench who built the equally historic Carey's Bay Pub – also with local stone. However, according to the present co-owner Annette Hayes, it is much older. It may have been started in the 1850s. Apparently the basement once had a tunnel running out to the wharf's edge for the purpose of transporting unwanted sailors and stowaways where they were locked in and manacled to the walls. This is a good story and not beyond the realms of possibility. In 1846 the NZ Company's Surveyor Charles Kettle arrived at what was then known as Koputai (Port Chalmers). He noted at the time that there seemed to be vast amounts of spirits and tobacco being brought in by visiting foreign ships. In 1844 a store and tavern was being operated by Octavius Harwood and by 1846 there were no fewer than six hotels operating at the Port of Otago. Local cabbage tree spirits and whisky distilled by David Carey and Charles Roebuck was reported as being a "fine drop". The first inn at the port was opened in 1844 by Alexander McKay and his wife Janet. It was known as the Surveyor's Arms and it provided accommodation and entertainment for surveyors, whalers and the few squatters around the harbour.

Strath Taieri

The Taieri plain was created by tectonic action and river deposits. The valley itself is a basin between two major fault lines along which block mountains (Rock and Pillar and Taieri Ridge) have risen. The hub of this area is the township of Middlemarch where this pub is situated, over the road from the railway station. Settlements such as this in Central Otago were created by either a gold rush or a land rush. Cottesbrook Station to the east of the village was first settled in 1856. Six years later it had an area of 12,500 hectares, carrying more than 3,000 diseased sheep. In 1868 William Gellibrand took over the run which had ballooned to almost 68,000 hectares, running 50,000 sheep and 537 cattle. Due to the remoteness of the station, the owner had great difficulty in disposing of surplus stock. During the 1870s sheep were being sold for sixpence each (5c) or simply driven over the nearest precipice!

Middlemarch is not named after a grand country home in Georgian, England, but because it formed "The March" (border between two large sheepstations). Early publicans to run this hotel were a Mr Simpson and a Mr Thayer. Today, Peter Hamer caters to the needs of the locals and, during the daylight saving hours, to the many hundreds of rail trippers who travel from Dunedin to Pukerangi and Middlemarch on the Taieri Gorge Railway excursion train, through country that can only be reached via the historic railway line.

The Criterion

This hotel, built in 1877, is administered by the Oamaru Whitestone Civic Trust. The Trust was formed in 1989 to purchase, restore and administer the wonderful buildings in the old town district which was originally grouped around the wharf and railway yards. How fortunate we are to have this example of our architectural heritage kept safe for future generations to enjoy.

On the day I made this drawing the pub was closed but I've promised myself that I will return to take a tincture or two within, and experience the ambience of those far off days.

Oamaru architects Forrester and Lemon were responsible for the design of this Victorian-Italiante style building. In 1906 the district went dry and it did not return to a "wet" state again until 1960 when a trust regime won the day by a mere 142 votes. This building has been a boarding house and storage for a foundry. It was also the site of the first agricultural and pastoral show held in the district in 1860. Above one of the doorways is the name of one of the early publicans – a Mr J. M. Brown who was also the licensee of the Star and Garter in 1891.

The Birthplace of a Motor Empire

Hotels and taverns of this design are not easy to make an attractive drawing of. The reason I have included it in this book is that it is situated in an area of considerable historical significance, pertaining to the story of motoring in New Zealand. I first found out about this history when I made a drawing of the old fellmongery in Heriot which I found to be the beginnings of the Todd Motor Empire.

Charles Todd Senior came to Dunedin from Scotland in the William Davie in 1870 and after moving from Milton to Tuapeka and Bendigo as a mine manager, he eventually settled in Heriot and established the fellmongery. His son, Charles Junior, joined him in this enterprise after leaving school in 1884 and for the next 31 years he was involved in storekeeping, auctioneering and sheep farming.

In 1912 he opened a small motor repair shop in the village, thus saving the few local motorists of the district a trip to Invercargill. The next move was to Dunedin to establish the stock and station firm of Todd Brothers Ltd. In 1923 he formed the Todd Motor Company after selling the stock and station firm to Dalgety and Company. In 1926 he moved to Wellington and by 1931 the Europa Oil Company was in operation.

The Todds imported their oil from Russia as it was by far the cheapest on the world market. When Charles Senior and Junior were laying the ground work of their empire in Heriot, the only pub was the Railway Hotel and one of the earliest licensees was Mr T. J. Collins. He advertised the fact that, "The hotel was but a chain [22 yards] from the railway station, is in a healthy climate and commands a magnificent view of the surrounding country. As well as first class tabling it has private suites for families with plunge and shower baths." It is doubtful that Charles Todd ever set foot in the hotel as he was an ardent teetotaller and a supporter of the Temperance Union. This did not preclude him and his family from being active in the sporting and social activities of this tiny settlement. Incidentally, my drawing of the fellmongery is now in the Todd Family Museum.

Hotel South Otago

The Clutha District was the first to vote for no licence in 1893 and by the time the newly elected trust members were coming to terms with what lay ahead, the district had been dry for 61 years. In 1955 the trust elected Mr R. G. Cullen as its first chairman and it immediately set about the vexed question of financing an operation which covered a large area, taking in Balclutha, Lawrence, Owaka, Clinton, Milton and Kaitangata – a daunting task and certainly not for the faint-hearted.

The government was the first to offer assistance in the form of a guaranteed overdraft of $14,000. Trading began immediately with the opening of bottle stores, but the locals made it quite clear that they wanted hotels and the sooner the better. A curious reaction came from the local bodies when they opposed the licensed trade's proposition of building 12 hotels in two electorates (Mataura and Clutha) on the grounds that they would have too much control over the sale of liquor! However, they seemed to have resolved that concern during the following years.

While yarning to Ken Wood, the licensee, he informed me that he leases the hotel from the trust – an idea that would be quite unfamiliar with a trust like Invercargill. This pub was originally an unlicensed private hotel of sturdy construction standing on a very commanding location just over the bridge going south.

Duntroon

James Little built an accommodation house in Duntroon in 1864 and a small town was born to service the needs of the Campbell Estate and others in the district. Duntroon was named after the birthplace of Robert Campbell who was born there in 1843. Campbell came to New Zealand in 1860 and rapidly became a large land-owner. On the Campbell Estate he built a 30 roomed baronial style limestone mansion at Otekaike where he died in 1889. A bequest left by his wife built St Martins Church in the village.

The Duntroon Tavern is one of the oldest existing hotels in the South Island mainly because of a roughcast coat applied over its weatherboards at some time in its long history. The concrete cladding certainly didn't enhance this fine old building but it may have saved it from fire which sadly destroyed the only other hotel to have traded in the district.

This pub became a tavern and restaurant in the late 1970s and when I made this drawing Liz and Keith Murray were the proprietors. Liz told me that they were shortly to give up the hotel life to find some normality in Oamaru after years of dealing with the public. "It will be a bit of a wrench," she told me because she had really enjoyed the history of the building. However, they had their eyes on an equally important and challenging historic home in Oamaru, which will, no doubt, keep them busy in the years to come.

Palmerston South

The old north western hotel stands at the junction of State Highway One and the legendary "Pigroot" which took the ever hopeful prospectors and no doubt some future publicans to the goldfields of the Maniototo in Central Otago. In 1883 there were eight hotels in this small town. This hotel was then being operated by Mr J. Thomson and all the usual names were given to the remaining seven, like Criterion, Palmerston, Carriers Arms, Waverley, Prince of Wales, Royal and the Empire. About this same time there were five milliners in town but only one hairdresser. Whoever that was must have been very busy at times or perhaps most of the cutting and styling was done at home. The number five appears again when counting the bootmakers. There were nine drapers and two dressmakers which indicates that fashionable dress and sturdy boots and shoes were not overlooked in this busy pioneer town 140 years ago. Palmerston's first sections were surveyed in 1864 and it became a municipality in 1872. If the street names look a little strange it's because they originated in the Orkney Islands where many of the new settlers originally came from. Runbrake Street and Tiverton Street got my attention.

The Outram Hotel

In 1891, Mr J. C. Johnston became the proprietor of the Outram Hotel. In that year he placed the following advertisement in Mills and Dick's Almanac and Directory.

"Since purchasing this old established hostelry I have thoroughly cleaned and repaired the premises inside and outside. Its accommodation is now unsurpassed, comprising luxurious bed and private sitting rooms, piano etc., with attendance if required. The cuisine is in the charge of an efficient chef and the general household management is under the immediate supervision of Mrs Johnston. Detached, commodious, well-lighted sample rooms, fitted with counters, shelves, seats and lamp for commercial travellers. Lock up coach house and loose box for entires or hunters. Good stabling with an experienced groom in attendance. Horses and buggies for hire. The wines, beers and spirits are the envy of connoisseurs and the cordials and liqueurs the most rabid teetotallers would enjoy. There are beautiful streams for trout fishing close by."

This rather florid description is typical of the time . . . but I was confused as to what the word "entires" meant in the context of a lockup coach house. Then along came a friend who informed me that an "entire" was an ungelded stallion that must be kept in a separate stall . . . Outram now services a farming area but was originally a staging post for the ever-hopeful miners on their way to the Central Otago diggings.

The Catlins Inn, Owaka

Prior to the prohibition era, 1904-54, Owaka had three hotels, Ford's Coffee Palace, with accommodation for 30 guests, the Railway and Vial's Catlins River Hotel which burned down in 1888. Owaka, which had several spellings during its history means "the place of the change". When the main trunk line between Dunedin and Invercargill was opened it seemed logical that a branch line from Balclutha through the Catlins to Tahakopa and Wyndham be investigated. Central Government became involved and it wasn't until they realised how important the timber from this region was that in 1885 it became a reality. The Catlins area as a tourist destination is becoming very popular because of its unique scenic beauty, and this Catlins Inn is more than able to cater for the hungry and thirsty traveller.

The Bowling Green

I arrived in Dunedin in 1951 and as my flatmate was a dental student, we had settled for a few rooms in Albany Street which meant that close by, were not only the medical and dental schools, but two other temples of temptation – the nurse's home and the Bowling Green Hotel, affectionately known as "The Bowler".

Ray Walker was the publican and very popular he was. One of my first seriously romantic adventures had its beginnings in the bar of this much loved pub. Years later I was regaled with the story of how I literally slid along the bar in a hazy state, to make the acquaintance of a young physiotherapy student who later became my wife.

Edward Holmes established this hotel on the corner of Cumberland and Frederick Streets in 1878 and was the licensee for the next three years. He then leased it to David Fergusson who stayed until 1885. In 1887 Edward Holmes returned to the corner but moved on again in 1899 never to return. In 1963 three members of the Auld family became the licensees and stayed for 20 years. Walter Digby Wyatt was the only proprietor to exceed this term of occupancy having served the public for 25 years between 1900 and 1925. From drawings made in the '60s I selected this one which is how I remember it. The large gin bottle on the roof was added much later, something I couldn't resist, if only to spice up some fairly boring architecture. It may not be an historic gem but it's certainly full of memories of a well-spent youth. It is now known as Zouga Ballantynes and the gin bottle has been replaced with a rampant elephant!

The "Glue Pot"

When first married I lived in one of a row of classic terraced houses in King Edward Street just a few doors along from Phil Ruston's Kensington Hotel, known to us locals as the "Glue Pot" in the early 1950s. That part of Dunedin was as close to Coronation Street as I ever got. The pub was almost next door, the movie theatre in the next block and all our shopping needs close by, including the corner shop right across the tram tracks. This hotel was established in 1874 by Timothy Hayes. It was apparently a popular venue for social occasions and was once the venue for an election meeting held by James Seaton who was campaigning for a seat on the Otago Provincial Council in 1875.

The day I made this drawing, the pub appeared to be deserted and looked rather sad, but on peering through the glass door for a moment or two, I could transport myself back 52 years and remember a leisurely drink or two on a Sunday morning – very illegal but so much more exciting than today.

The Mornington Hotel

The present Mornington Tavern came into being as a result of a syndicate formed in 1971 to establish an hotel at 36 Mailer Street, Dunedin. In 1974 the licence of the Newtown Tavern in Matakanui was transferred to Mornington where a tavern has been operating ever since. This drawing of the Mornington Hotel has a somewhat different history. Matthew Fogarty was the licensee between 1871 and 1875 and, as you will see, it was also the clubrooms of the Dunedin Golf Club. I don't know of any other hotel which has acted in this capacity but it must have been a jolly "tenth hole" on occasions (it was a nine hole course).

This hotel was situated on the corner of Meadow Street and Parkhill Avenue. It was rebuilt in 1871 and demolished in 1976. In 1873 a Scot by the name of Charles Ritchie-Howden rejuvenated the golf club which was moved to a new site above the Roslyn Woollen Mills and from there, to its present home at Balmacewen.

The Crown Hotel

This is one of the oldest established hotels in Dunedin beginning its long life in 1862 under the guidance of David White. When he applied for licence in April of that year it was granted with certain conditions outlined by Police Inspector Weldon at the Annual Licensing Committee Meeting. He told Mr White "that as his 'house' was very small it would only be licensed to sell beer and wine, but not spirits."

When this pub was established there were three hotels on the corner of MacLaggan and Rattray Streets – the Shakespeare (sometimes spelt "Shakspere"), the Shamrock and the Crown. It began, as many of Dunedin's pubs did, as a small wooden building. It was later replaced with a fine brick structure which housed a dining, commercial, reading and billiard room. The bars were on the ground floor as they are today and upstairs were 30 bedrooms.

Among the publicans were the Branson Brothers in 1928-29. Branson's Hotel in St Andrew Street still trades after 132 years. This pub was operated by Charles Branson in 1897 who was, I presume, the father of the Branson Brothers. From 1959 to 1966, Jack, the father of Literary Notable Bill Manhire, was the licensee of this hotel. He and his wife Maisie were well known and respected publicans in various pubs in the south.

The Rugby

Perched precariously on the southwest corner of Hope and Carrol Streets stands the Rugby Hotel which began its life as the Caledonian. From 1863, when it was established till 1868, William Christie was mine host, followed in 1868 by William Fraser. The last publican of the Caledonian era was P. V. Stevens who reigned until 1924 when the name was changed to Rugby. In 1957 it was renamed the Masonic but in 1982 they changed the name back to the Rugby. A pub of many names!

In 1880 John Ogg established another Caledonian Hotel. This was the Caledonian Grounds Hotel. Annie Blaney was the licensee between 1906 and 1912. She later became hostess of Tatts Hotel which was commonly known as "Ma Blaney's" in my days in Dunedin. The Rugby was originally of wooden construction and like many others it was destroyed by fire in 1874. Bill Skitch was one of the personalities who ran this pub between 1904 and 1907. He was a foundation member of the Dunedin Cricket Club and a member of the Otago Cricket Association for many years. No doubt there were many hundreds of cricket strokes played and overs bowled, along with the mass of statistics argued about, in the bar of this hotel all those years ago.

The Law Courts

This hotel stands on the corner of Stuart and Cumberland Streets amidst some of the most beautiful buildings in the city. When I came to Dunedin in 1951 it was only a short walk from the magnificent railway station which faced the red brick police station and barracks and the highly decorative court house.

Thankfully most of the old buildings in the area have been carefully maintained. The Law Courts Hotel was established by William Fidler in 1863 and was named the Auld Scotland Hotel. In 1902 it was renamed the Law Courts for obvious reasons.

Alexander Stewart took over in 1913 and remained there as owner and licensee until the end of World War II in 1945. Running a hotel during World War I and World War II must have presented a few problems for the publicans of the day. A dire shortage of spirits was just one of the many impositions but no doubt there was a plentiful supply of the local brew – the renowned Speights ale! The chef must have been innovative too, coping with the rationing of butter, sugar and meat, but menus were far simpler then, weren't they. Part of this building was demolished in 1937, rebuilt in stone and transformed into one of the most modern hotels of its kind in New Zealand.

The Royal Albert

During my early days in Dunedin this was one of the more popular student haunts known affectionately as the "R.A.". Because of the way Dunedin's streets dart hither and yon at all angles, this pub looks like the front of a naval destroyer. This is just one of the reasons why I love this city. The pubs are built to fit into and on top of some of the steepest, winding streets in New Zealand.

The first hotel on this corner of George and London Streets was established in 1864 and was known as the Black Bull. In 1880 Daniel White took over the licence and changed the name to the Royal Albert – probably to honour the consort of Queen Victoria. In 1860 Daniel White was listed as the proprietor of the Epicurean Restaurant in McLaggan Street. From there he became the temporary licensee of the Commercial Inn which, according to the *Otago Witness* of 1851, was the first hotel established in Dunedin by Tom Watson in June 1848. We spent many happy hours in the "R.A." in the '50s and across the road stood our Sunday afternoon refuge, the Robbie Burns. In those days Sunday drinking was a dangerous pursuit and I can well remember many hasty exits just ahead of the law, all adding to the excitement of a young man's life – the equivalent of today's boy racers I suppose . . .

St Kilda Hotel

In 1891 there were 81 hotels listed in the *Dunedin Business Directory*. The St Kilda Hotel was opened in 1873 by John Pugh Jones, a Welshman, who arrived in Dunedin in 1859. His original trade, which he no doubt plied in his native Wales, was shoemaking or cobbling as it was once known. He opened a shop in Carrol Street, later moving to the corner of Prince Albert and Bay View Roads where he began hotel keeping. This fellow must have had more than a slight interest in community affairs because in 1875 he stood for and was elected the first mayor of St Kilda in those far off days when each suburban community in a city had its own administration. When I arrived in Invercargill in the mid '50s, South Invercargill had its own council. Time may have centralised the administration of cities but there now seems to be more bureaucrats than ever before. Such is progress.

When I was carousing around Dunedin the proprietor of this pub was William Massetti, son of Severio, who was the licensee from 1938 to 1943 and again in 1946. Like the Brun family in Queenstown's Mountaineer Hotel in the 1950s, the Massettis were very obviously European with swarthy good looks and genial demeanor.

I can well remember travelling around the city's hotels in whatever tram was available. We could comfortably visit four or five hotels by climbing on a Number 7 St Kilda tram in the exchange without fear of being breathalised! St Kilda, "The Western Land", an island of six square miles in the outer Hebrides, was evacuated in 1930. The 36 inhabitants were taken (at their request) to Morven County Argyll. Unlike Dunedin's St Kilda it is now seldom visited.

The Fitzroy

In 1984 the "Fitz" celebrated its centenary. This pub was established by John McKersey but little more is known of its early history. McKersey was the licensee for only two years when Jane Ingram took over and it is interesting to note that in this day and age we do tend to think that the fair sex are only just getting a foothold in managing the nation's economy. Looking back over my research I find just how wrong some of us are in this supposition because, as far back as the 1860s, women ran hotels such as the Miss Stanley's at Macraes Flat, Mrs O'Meara at the Supreme Court Hotel in Queenstown, Mrs McBride's hotel also in Queenstown, Mrs Bond at the Mountaineer at Queenstown, Mrs Callaghan who ran the Shamrock at Fairfax, and more recently the indominable Peg Taylor at Ohai and Peg Newman at Parawa to name a few.

Up until 1984 the Fitzroy had 28 licensees, Jack Doyle hosting for the longest period at 14 years.

It is also well known for its support of local sports clubs such as Southern Rugby, Fitzroy Netball, and the Rajahs Softball Club. Situated at 469 Hillside Road the property was originally known as the Fitzroy Estate.

The Clarendon

This very Australian looking hotel was originally situated at the junction of Rattray Street and MacLaggan Streets and in 1862 was known as the Shamrock. In 1902 the licence was transferred to a new site on the corner of Clark and MacLaggan Streets – this was a large, two-storeyed building. The proprietors, C. F. and C. J. Hartnett, renamed the hotel in 1936 as the Clarendon and a handsome building it is too. The view from the balcony is a bonus. The views from the hills of Dunedin are one of the many facets of this city which has made it my favourite of the cities I've lived in. Since the days of the Shamrock a few of the proprietors have been Donald Murphy who established it in 1862, Thomas Hetherington 1874-86, yet another hostess Janet Gebbie in 1884-90 and William Coughlan. Since the hotel was shifted to its present location complete with name change, some of the hosts have been Mary Campbell, Mrs G. F. Hartnett, Estaban Marquex and Carl Larsen who I think ran a hotel in Levin in the 1950s when I lived there.

Among the strange names given the watering holes in Dunedin in the 1860s was an hotel near the Crown in MacLaggan Street, with the name Bull and Mouth. Others I found were Water of Leith, Spread Eagle, Steam Packet, Shakspere (note the spelling), Robin Hood, Odd Whim and the Hit or Miss. Yes, they are weird but they really existed.

Prince of Wales

1886 heralded the opening of this hotel established by George Davis who had previously operated a pub in the Victorian goldfields. It proved very popular with the many thousands of Australian miners who flocked to the Central Otago diggings. Originally it was built of timber but when Bob Waters and Mick Ryan took over, they set about building a substantial hotel in 1876 which has survived till this day. I can well remember the days when in 1976 Carnarvon Hotels Ltd decided to build a restaurant on the first floor which featured an 1873 steam locomotive complete with two carriages and a guard's van. The engine and carriages were set on real railway lines complete with ballast and served as dining cars.

I once played in a band here and live music was a regular feature of this popular venue. Among the many proprietors there have been a number of Scots, Irish and a sprinkling of ladies such as Ellen Tully and Janet Hinchcliff but the exception was in 1883-85 when Bonifacio Zurari hosted this hotel. Could he have been Italian?

The Empire

The first hotel in this site at 400 Princes Street was the Queen's Arms which was opened by Mr J. W. Feger in 1858, making it one of Dunedin's earliest hotels. One rather unusual event took place in this hotel. The second only Catholic Mass held in Dunedin was celebrated in this hotel followed by the third at which Father Petitjean was the celebrant, in a bottle store owned by a brewer by the name of Burke. In its early days it was known as the Queen's Arms Coffee and Dining Rooms. Tea and coffee was priced at three pence (6c) and, if required, a plate of bread and butter at no extra charge. Board and lodging could be obtained at 20 shillings ($2) a week.

When this hotel was known as the Union, after 1891, yet another lady was the licensee. In 1891 Elizabeth Colville was the hostess followed in 1892 by Johanna McLean. This building was used as an hotel continuously for 140 years before it closed in 1999. It had been a live music venue in the '80s and '90s hosting bands such as The Chills, Verlaines and The Clean. In 2005 the Empire was bought by two English backpackers, Kate Kavanagh and Lucy Hobbs, who have brought it back to life.

The Waterloo

The Crossan family had a 46 year association with this hotel which was originally known as Searle's Hotel when George Searle was the owner between 1889-1906. Bill, Ellen and Gladys Crossan all took turns as licensees of this historic pub.

In 1952 Walter Heeney assumed control of the Waterloo but before Bill Crossan finally broke the family chain he held an "open house" for his regulars.

The news travelled fast and in a short time the bars were full to overflowing. Every manner of beer, wine and spirts were dispensed free of charge and in an hour or so the Waterloo was a "Pub with no Beer". Extensive alterations were carried out in 1967 when Fred La Hood took over the licence. This hotel had its beginnings on Ruskin Terrace, Forbury Corner, in 1883 under the ownership of John T. Sneade. Since 1883 this pub has had more than 30 proprietors.

The Parkside at Caversham

On many occasions in the 1950s I crammed into the bar of this hotel and drank to both victory and defeat. That's the good thing about toasting the aftermath of a game of rugby in Otago – whatever the outcome we drink the amber liquid! This pub, situated at 147 South Road, was established by John Hammell in 1863. The original structure was of wood and stone and single storeyed. It was next door to a blacksmith's shop operated in 1880 by William Read. Then along came Matthew Dawson who began his hotel career in the bustling town of Cromwell in 1892, moving to Dunedin in 1905 to begin a 30 year stay during which time this present building replaced the old. Once again we note that among the 14 licensees, three were women — Elizabeth Messent in 1946-48, Annie Cuthbert 1951-52 and Avis Muirhead 1960-63. In the 1800s the Dunedin suburbs were very self contained. For instance, there were two breweries, one of which was run by James Briggs in Sydney Street. His brew was called "Standard" and his advertisement of the day proclaimed that his ales and stout were awarded three prizes at the New Zealand and South

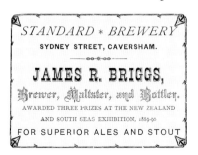

Seas Exhibition 1889-90. The other brewery was operated by Cowie and Company. There were four drapers, four market gardeners, five bootmakers and five butchers – all this in Caversham in 1890 . . .

The White Horse at Becks

I walked into the bar of the new White Horse on the first Sunday of duckshooting. Gary and Karen George were standing in the middle of a deserted bar looking quite dazed. I asked them how long they had been in the hotel business and Karen answered with a wry grin that this was day four. "We've had duckshooters wall to wall since day one and this is our first opportunity to take stock and work out what it's all about."

Gary and Karen took over "the Horse" after living in the former Methodist Church at Coal Creek for the past five years. "From saints to sinners," said Gary. Before this couple took over, the pub was closed for two months and there was a collective sigh of relief from the locals when their pub was returned to them.

Across the road stands the now restored Old White Horse lovingly cared for by the local historical society. In 1864, John Nixon Beck established the hotel as a coaching stop to cater for the travellers to and from the Central Otago goldfields. The wooden section was a later addition and when completed the hotel comprised 10 bedrooms, two sitting rooms, a commodious dining room and kitchen and seating to cater for 16 guests. In 1878 a post office was added, then in 1896 a telephone exchange was established.

Robert Mee, whose family still farms in the district, became the proprietor in 1909 then built the "New Hotel" in 1925. The history of the hotels span 141 years from goldmining to farming.

"Vulcan, the God of Fire . . ."

When I first laid eyes on St Bathans in the early 1950s there were quite a few more buildings in the narrow, winding street. I can't for the life of me find those early drawings and I don't have a photo because in those days I didn't own a camera. I do wish I could describe them for you but you will have to make do with what I offer.

This is my favourite view of the Vulcan seen as I walk up from that astonishing man-made lake – the Blue Lake – which is very blue some days and rather dull on others. Over the years I've drawn almost every building in this historic treasure tucked away under Mt St Bathans where in 1864 gold was discovered.

The story of the Vulcan and the Ballarat are entwined and make quite a story. The original Vulcan was built of corrugated iron in 1869, quite a distance from the present site. It was owned by Samuel Hanger, the village blacksmith and I can only hazard a guess that he was a knowledgeable chap who named his pub after the mythical Roman god of fire and metallurgy which neatly fitted his occupation. But I'm only guessing. By 1881 the town had outgrown the tin shed and Samuel then rebuilt in sun-dried bricks but this one was destroyed by fire in 1914 and was replaced by a red brick structure. Yet again fire struck the Vulcan (well named by this time) and the licence was transferred to the now vacant Ballarat Hotel, named I presume after the Australian goldfield, by a Mr P. Hanrahan. This was built in 1882 of mud bricks and stands proudly today as the fifth Vulcan. If you haven't visited this little historic corner of Otago you are certainly missing a treat. Go to the Vulcan and have a yarn to mine host Mike Cavanagh.

The Lauder Tavern

The first drink I had in this 101-year-old pub was in 1952 when it was across the road facing the railway. In 1904 Daniel Joseph Donnelly and Charles Waide Jnr applied for a hotel licence. The licence was granted on the condition that it would be completed by 1 July 1904 and it was, a first class, 16 bedroom hotel.

It then became a victim of the great railway demolition and in 1961 it was shifted over to face the main road.

In 1908 the proprietor George McCluskey was declared bankrupt and Elizabeth Donnelly took over. I assume Elizabeth was the wife or daughter of Daniel Joseph.

In 1912, according to a court report, Elizabeth was charged with permitting drunkenness on her premises. "Several testified to seeing John Allen, half sprung, fighting the air and Charles Deal was seen lying outside the hotel with his clothes on fire!" This could have come from a Monty Python script.

Among the many licensees down through the ages were John Ryan who came down the road from Naseby, Mick O'Brien, Jim Looney, Phil McEldowney and in 1912 Dan Donnelly made another appearance at Lauder. The Irish seemed to be in full force at times during the early days of this pub. The day I went back to make myself known prior to making a serious start on this book, I found Karen mopping out after a weekend assault by duck shooters, the co-owner Robin was in the kitchen. I thank them for their help.

Cape Broome

This is a familiar sight to travellers from south on their way to the "Heart of the Desert" – Central Otago. It's the remains of the Cape Broome Hotel which dates back to the 1860s gold era. The district is known as Fruitlands but originally it was called Bald Hill.

After World War I the area started out with a flourish of trumpets with the promise of a big commercial apple growing project. Several prominent Dunedin businessmen invested heavily but found to their horror, after a couple of crops, that the area was prone to severe late frosts. A fierce freeze in year three killed the fruit before it had formed and the trees were hauled out and the 60 acre blocks were sold to the recently returned servicemen for dairying.

I have always imagined that this fine octagonal stone building was the hotel's original dairy and storehouse. It's a wonderful example of the Cornish stonemason's art, many of which are still standing. According to my records the then empty hotel was used to store the few apples that were harvested from the ill-fated project. We are indeed fortunate that so many of these relics have been preserved in this high, dry climate.

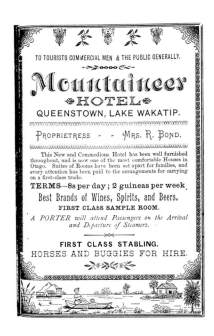

Parts of Old Queenstown Survive

My late friend and colleague F. W. G. Miller once wrote about this drawing of the Mountaineer Hotel which I made in the early 70s ". . . that there is a timelessness about Queenstown despite the new high rise buildings which are the hallmark of the tourist boom. It is this timelessness, of course, which has helped to create this tourist boom, causing the new buildings to crowd in and obstruct the old."

Fortunately some of the old landmarks, other than those fashioned by nature, remain and it is these old buildings that give this lakeside town much of its charm. I wonder what my old friend would think of this tourist town now.

When I first crossed the threshold of this hotel it was a real pub with a genuine smoky atmosphere. At the helm was the legendary "Poppa Brun" and his family. I was at this time briefly employed by the distributors of a well known French brandy to travel the length and breadth of Central Otago painting point of sale displays in the many hotels. I was a 23-year-old, living the good life and when I wrote to my father and told him what I was doing he wrote back saying, "The Lord has indeed smiled upon you my son . . ." Thank goodness it was only a temporary job!

My main memory of the job was that I disposed of my salary in a most undignified way. How I worked during the day I don't quite know but I do think that instinct had a lot to do with it.

I still take a brandy or two on occasions . . .

John Marsh's Hotel, Cromwell

Fred Miller and I stayed overnight at this hotel soon after it was announced that the Clyde Dam project was to go ahead. If I remember correctly, Social Credit's Gary Knapp and Bruce Beetham swung the vote in Parliament. The year was 1974 and Fred and I had decided that he, an historian and ex-goldminer, and me, an artist who was passionate about "The Heart of the Desert", should start a book to commemorate the history and romance of this great little town. It was to be titled *Cromwell*. Fred and I had contributed a weekly Saturday column to *The Southland Times* for 22 years – a drawing and a story – so it was not difficult for us to make the decision to record in picture and word the buildings that were about to disappear under the waters of this harsh land.

We imagined that after all the clamour and opposition from the environmentalists and other pressure groups we would be embarking on a worthwhile project. But, how wrong can you be! It wasn't until years later when the book was out of print that any interest was shown.

However, to get back to the night at the Cromwell Hotel. We mingled with the locals in the public bar before and after a very plain but hearty hotel meal we met some real characters, among them being a brash young political hopeful by the name of Ian Quigley who stood for and won the Otago Central seat for Labour in 1972. The following election, another young aspirant from the other side of the political world by the name of Warren Cooper took all before him and finished up as the "Minister of Warren Affairs", as we affectionately dubbed him in those days.

I've more to say about the Cooper dynasty later in the book – namely his irascible father, the legendary "Wicked Willy" of McBride's Hotel in Queenstown.

Rae's Junction

When you are travelling to Central Otago from Invercargill via Tapanui or from Dunedin via Milton, you must pass the neat red brick hotel at the junction of Stage Highways 8 and 90. I checked in my Mills and Dick and Company's almanac and directory of 1891 and found that this hotel was listed as the Junction Hotel. At the junction of Switzers and Teviot Roads – far more romantic sounding than a simple highway number.

Isla Rae was the proprietress and she boasted "Ample accommodation for travellers, excellent stabling, every attention to horses and, wines, spirts and ales of the best qualities."

Other services offered in this village was the post office (run by Isla) and the local J.P. by the name of James Bennett. The only evidence of a postal service these days is the row of letterboxes at the corner. The first time I stopped off for a beer, many years ago, a local shearing gang were in residence. They filled the whole bar!

Memories of Coaching Days

In 1953 I was on my way back from Middlemarch via Macraes Flat when I stopped to draw the deserted Alexandra Hotel between Dunback and Palmerston on the Pigroot Road. This is indeed a relic of the coaching days when there were at least 80 hotels on this stretch of road. For the coaches, gold escorts and thousands of prospectors on their way inland, a hotel a day's walk from the previous one was a must. It's hard to imagine how busy and exciting these goldfield trails must have been in the 19th century in Otago. This hotel was large by the standards of the day with plenty of accommodation and of sturdy construction.

The name Pigroot was given to this road by a surveyor who also named Hogburn, Sowburn, Gimmerburn, Wedderburn and Kyeburn, after animals. It is said that his original list was an excellent one, embodying local characteristics and Maori lore but an unimaginative senior at head office found the names hard to pronounce and sent it back to him with the instructions to be more practical. So in high dudgeon he submitted, as a gesture of protest the names listed above – and they were accepted! Nothing much has happened at head offices among the bureaucrats in the intervening years has it? A few months ago I went back to this spot to find only the remains of the lower floor still standing – methinks the result of a fire.

A Victim of the Clyde Dam

The Welcome Home Hotel once stood opposite the Lowburn Bridge on the road to Wanaka and Hawea. The district was known as Lowburn Ferry and it is now underwater. This pub was built in 1869 and was established originally to cater for those travellers waiting to be ferried across the mighty Clutha which I guess could be a scary venture on occasions. This was the third building on this site – each one being rebuilt within the same metre-thick walls.

In 1878 the Clutha flooded and invaded the building through the front door leading to one intrepid drinker to row his boat inside and up to the bar, but even more bizarre was the resident goat who regularly lined up for a tipple. A great favourite of the locals for many years.

The ferry ceased in 1938 when M.P. Bill Bodkin opened the bridge which was proudly proclaimed as the longest bridge in the world. It was unique in as much as the hump in the middle precluded one from seeing the other end. It was a very hot day in 1974 when I drew this pub and I was glad to partake of a few cool "quiets" when I finished drawing this utilitarian structure.

The Original Royal

This was the original Royal Hotel in Naseby and when I made this drawing in 1977 and published it in *The Southland Times* no one believed that such a small building could have functioned as an hotel. They obviously didn't know that in 1883 there were nine hotels in this busy mining town. In 1863 there were more than 5,000 thirsts to quench. The only other diversion from working and drinking was a billiard hall in the Ancient Briton Hotel which doubled as a doctor's surgery for those who injured themselves during the sometimes dangerous business of mining for the elusive gold or fell foul of the bad whisky which brought about "delirium tremens". Mercifully the modern day liquor hasn't the poisonous properties of the "firewater" of old, when just a modest amount would render the most mild-mannered man positively dangerous to be around.

In the early 1800s a Mr E. Horswell was mine host in this unpretentious little watering hole. I've been back recently to make a drawing of the present day Royal which is just around the corner from Strong's Watchmakers shop which has been lovingly maintained for more than 140 years.

The Present Royal

The Coat of Arms of this hotel sits proudly on the verandah of this Naseby pub, complete with the motto of the Royal Arms of Great Britain "Dieu et Mon Droit" (God and My Right). When these hotels were established it was fashionable to show one's loyalty to the Crown. How many Royal hotels have you been in throughout the Commonwealth? Now a Royal tour is practically ignored by Australians and New Zealanders as we drift towards becoming a republic. For history's sake I hope we don't completely do away with those names that live on like Prince of Wales, Victoria, Duke of Wellington, The Royal and The Crown.

The first drawing I made of this old pub was of the side alley with its empty barrels and stacks of crates. I don't think it went down too well all those years ago when it was published in *The Southland Times*. "Why draw the bloody backyard?" was one of the comments made at the time.

History Side by Side, Lee Stream

On the road to Middlemarch between Outram and Clark's Junction lies this collection of buildings from another time. I made this drawing in 1988. Much earlier I had partaken of an ale or two (I think it was in the late '50s) in the more modern and rather boring hotel on the left.

While I was drawing this little settlement I sensed I was being watched and it turned out that someone had taken up residence in the dry hotel. I have found out very little about this traveller's rest but I can imagine it would be a very busy place during the gold rush days. The road originally ran right past the doors of the buildings but nowadays the modern highway allows you to look down on this little cluster of history.

Stanley's Hotel, Macraes Flat

"'Twas a dark and stormy night . . ." So began many a poem – good and bad – but it is the perfect opening for this tale which begins in 1953 when a friend and I were on our way to Middlemarch via the Pigroot and the high road to Macraes Flat. It had begun to snow soon after we reached Dunback and by the time we had fortuitously reached Stanley's Hotel at Macraes it had become impossible to proceed. And so that is how I came to spend a night with the Misses Stanley at their stone hotel in the middle of nowhere.

My abiding memory of this night, 50 years ago, were the starched white cotton sheets on my single bed. The risk of frost-bite was averted by a hot water bottle and the thought of a hearty breakfast the following freezing morning made this unplanned break in the journey (in a 1937 Chevrolet) well worthwhile.

This pub, like many others that began their lives in the 19th century, has a wonderful history which began with a rush for gold in 1868 followed by the rebuilding of the hotel in 1882 by Tom Stanley who employed the legendary "Budge" who was not only a craftsman of high repute but also an unsurpassed drinker of ale. He agreed to be paid in the local brew which I presume also included a bunk and a crust of bread. It took him five years to build this fine hotel and the final reckoning revealed that he had drunk 72 hogsheads (17,200 litres) and that he was still in Tom Stanley's debt! Above the door, in true English style, is a crest showing a rampant rooster proclaiming that "While I live I crow". I have spent many months in the past 30 years painting and drawing in this district thanks to the hospitality of a dear friend and local runholder, John Sutton of Doch Royle Station. These days the area is a very different place with the Gargantuan gold mining project dominating the landscape – but that is another very long story.

The Victoria

Known in 1883 as the Victoria Junction Hotel it still stands on the highest point of what used to be the main drag in Cromwell's Melmore Terrace. It's the only one to survive the flooding of this historic precinct. Its licensee in 1883 was Mr J. Stuart.

Other hotels of the time were the Bridge, the Junction Commercial, White Hart, Golden Age, the Globe and the Temperance. There was an interesting line-up of storekeepers in the 1880s. I. Hallenstein & Co., D. A. Jolly & Co., Sherwood & Co., and Kum Goon W.A. & Co. were the movers and shakers of the commercial world.

Once again we witness the fact that the only buildings to survive more than 140 years have been the pubs, the churches and the odd lodge temple. The pioneers certainly got their priorities right, didn't they!

One of the First to Disappear

When I was in Cromwell drawing the buildings that were due to be submerged all those years ago this stable was standing with its back to the river across from the Railway Road Services Depot. In 1883 when John Marsh was mine host of the Hotel Cromwell, these stables were only a few steps from his front door. This was Cobb & Co's depot and many a weary traveller stretched their aching legs after a long, bumpy trip from Dunedin or wherever and made a beeline for the bar, the dining room or the bedroom or all three in this order. The stables were built in 1866 by Cobbs, the famous coaching firm that was known throughout Australia and New Zealand. From this building walked many a celebrity of the day, among those being the famous English author Anthony Trollope. I wonder what his first impression was when he had taken in this mining town and its surrounding barren, rocky landscape.

Maniototo, Art Deco

I can remember when opposing international rugby teams got together after the match either under the stand or at their hotel and began, in some instances, lifelong friendships. Sadly the professional era has put a stop to most of that for all but the stage-managed press conferences. Luckily, rugby at club level still seems to have retained what rugby was all about – a good hard game and when it's over, all is forgiven and comradeship and the game become the most important thing. Rugby and country pubs are synonymous. One of my most treasured memories is of the day I wandered into this pub and spotted a face I recognised immediately. The year was 1953 and this fellow had recently been to South Africa as an All Black and had played in three of the four tests – we lost all four! His name? J. C. (Snow) Kearney who wore the black shirt on 22 occasions between 1947 and 1949 against Australia and South Africa. Snow was not only a competent midfield back but also a magnificent drop kick exponent. He played his club rugby for Ranfurly along with another stalwart of the game, W. A. Meates, and of course many times for Otago. Our conversation, fuelled with the amber fluid, was long and animated as the afternoon wore on and then, quite out of the blue, a group from *The Otago Daily Times* arrived and among them was yet another fellow I had admired for many a long day, in the form of Sid Scales – one of New Zealand's foremost cartoonists.

The day and night was long and eventful and I often reflect on the sheer coincidence of two people I admired so greatly just happened to be in this splendid art deco pub in the middle of the Maniototo on the same day as me.

In 1933 the town was almost completely destroyed by fire, in 1934 this fine hotel was rebuilt in the art deco style – a style that a number of other buildings in the township adopted and the reason that Ranfurly now hosts an annual "Art Deco Festival". People from far and near flock to this celebration of cars, music and buildings. Like Napier, out of a tragedy came a celebration of an architectural style, wonderfully stylish clothes and music to match.

Commercial Hotel, Omakau

This fine building was established in 1898 by William Leask. The first time I took a sip or two in this pub was on the occasion of the local race meeting. When we had absorbed all the atmosphere and fluids in the Commercial we then crossed the river to brighten up the lives of Kevin and Brida Dowling at the Black's Hotel. I don't recall we made any money but the size of our bets wouldn't have brought about mass insolvency. If you are in this neighbourhood during early January you will be treated to harness and galloping racing at this very old racing club. The Omakau Racing Club was alive and well in 1891. The president was J. C. Jones who was also the local flour miller. There were three hotels: Blacks, where mine host was J. W. McIntosh; the Shamrock, where Mrs Gavin reigned and Mr Ryan's Bendigo. In the late 1800s Blacks (which was renamed Omakau when the railway went through) had many meanings. Among them was the name "wading-place" presumably because it was a place to cross over the Manuherikia River to Ophir which still boasts a classic restored Victorian post office and a now disused court house, both of which I have made many drawings. It's interesting to note in the early business directories which I refer to regularly, that many of the local gentry were multi-talented. For instance, John McKnight was the local wheelwright, coachbuilder and undertaker and, believe it or not, this tiny goldfield town had John W. Moore the tailor to keep all and sundry looking neat and fashionable at weddings, funerals and important social occasions.

Father Sheehan and the Rev. Henry had a hand in the births, marriages and deaths of the good folk of Ophir and Omakau as did Dr Hyde who no doubt had more than his share of Jekyll and Hyde jokes . . . William Hurston Leask established this hotel in 1898 as Pomona House. William was born at Pomona in the Orkney Islands in 1836. He immigrated to New Zealand in about 1860 and had a successful gold mine, "Blacks Diggings", in 1863.

In 1903 the rail came to Omakau and the guests at the opening were fêted at Pomona House.

In 1926 The Duke of York visited this grand hotel. The present licensees are Mike and Mirka Jennings who took over from Murray and Cheryl Hall. On my last visit to the pub it was awash with cyclists of all ages who were taking a break from the now famous Rail Trail.

Black's Hotel

In 1883 Mr J. W. McIntosh was busy rebuilding his hotel – for the third time – in stone. He was taking no chances! Today there is nothing left of this unlucky pub which once stood down the road near the perfectly preserved Ophir Post Office building. Ophir's other claim to fame is the fact that the area has recorded the lowest winter temperatures ever experienced in New Zealand. This pub was built in 1937 and is currently owned and operated by Tom Rutherford. Like the commercial over the bridge in Omakau it shows signs of art deco design, as does the Garston, Benmore and Ranfurly Hotels. In early January the Omakau Racing Club hosts the racing fraternity at their annual two day galloping and harness meeting. It is generally hot, the tourists are on the move and I found when I attended many years ago that for many people it is the only race meeting they ever attend. Horse racing with a holiday atmosphere, and you can barely see the hotel for cars and people. The crowds eventually depart and it's back to its usual quiet, friendly, idyllic state. This is a wonderful little corner of Otago.

The Stables at Matakanui

This wonderfully preserved building, standing behind the historic general store must have been a hive of equine industry in the mining days. No doubt the travellers who stayed at the Newtown Hotel stabled their steeds in these loose boxes constructed of sun-dried brick and roofed with corrugated iron which, even after a hundred years shows virtually no rust. The combination of high altitude and dry climate has been kind to many Central Otago buildings.

Newtown Tavern, Matakanui

This hotel was rebuilt in 1913 when the settlement was still referred to as Tinkers. There seems to be a certain amount of confusion as to the names of these villages so I will quote from the local business directory of 1883. The Matakanui Hotel was kept by the postmaster and storekeeper Mr Henry Duck at Drybread.

According to legend it was known as the "Blue Duck" for obvious reasons. In the same year Mrs Mellor ran the post office and the Newtown Hotel. In 1891 the Newtown was operated by Robert Sheppard who was also the storekeeper at Tinkers. Tinkers was named for two itinerant tinsmiths who struck it rich while prospecting in this area.

Robert Sheppard was mine host from 1887 till 1895 when he sold to William Wall who reigned over this tiny principality until 1904. After a succession of owners it seems that Thomas Truedale sold this hotel to Felix Donnelly in 1926. Felix and his wife Grace ran this isolated pub until the late '60s – this must be the longest hotel tenure in Central Otago. When the licence was transferred to the Mornington Tavern in Dunedin in 1974 Felix and Grace stayed on in the pub – Felix tending a few sheep on his 300 acres. He was 82 when the licence ceased and when asked about retirement, he reminded us that he had worked hard all his life, including working as a gold miner for a shilling (10c) a day. The bar in this hotel was one of the smallest in Central Otago measuring 14 feet by 8 feet. Only the original Chatto Creek bar was smaller.

Felix converted a storeroom into his Duckshooter's Bar, thus enabling them to accommodate 100 patrons. I remember the small bar where I took refreshments, when, in the '60s, I first drew and painted the historic stables and store. Felix really packed them in each Easter when he accommodated the Zingari Rugby Club who came up to do battle with Matakanui. Felix's brothers, Frank, George and Jack played for Matakanui and in the 1920s represented Otago.

The Ancient Briton, Naseby

In 1883 it was written of Naseby that "about one thousand pounds ($2,000) has been expended in the efforts to discover a deep lead of gold – a depth of 350 feet has been reached and promising indications encourage the continuation of the work which is being continued by public efforts. Mr Hjorring has erected large and handsome new drapery premises, Mr Law, a new and solid butchering premises, and Mr Eccles a new hotel in place of that destroyed by fire." Incidentally Mr Eccles' hotel was one of nine operating at the time of the gold rush. Mr R. Webber was the proprietor of the Ancient Briton in those days. In 1891 John Fergusson was mine host of this hotel which along with the Royal are the only two survivors of the licensed trade in Naseby – now a popular tourist destination. This hotel was built shortly after the gold rush in 1863 and a room upstairs became Naseby's first surgery.

It is recorded that the billiard room was used for this purpose prior to the hospital being established some time before 1883. The resident surgeon was Dr James Whitton M.D. who may well have performed his profession in this hotel. A sport that has been synonymous with Naseby down through the years to this day is the very theatrical art of curling. This hotel is the headquarters of the Otago Central Curling Club and the Pioneer Curling Club. When I first witnessed this sport I looked around the rink here in Naseby and thought – "Only this could happen in such a setting . . ."

On one of my many visits to this village I spent an hour in the bar and met a fellow by the name of Ross McMillan, a poet who publishes under the *nom de plume* of "Blue Jeans" – I bought a book of his poems and we had a few more beers . . . Twenty-five years later I was gifted a new edition of Ross's work by a high country runholder friend from neighbouring Macraes Flat. I decided I would make contact with Ross again to glean an anecdote or two from him about the Ancient Briton where, in his own words "I've been known to have a few beers over the years . . ."

Today when the lazy wind wanders down the street and pushes the door of the bar wide open – then lets it shut, the locals look at each other knowingly and observe – "It's only Charlie's Ghost". Charlie Knowles was one of the town's real characters, who, along with "Hoofie" were among the regulars at the Brit. in the '50s when Tom Stocktill was mine host. Stocky was a hard case who drank a lot of brandy and port. During his years behind the bar, six o'clock closing ruled a lot of lives. It's recorded that a number of the town's wives complained to their local copper, Constable Fowler, that their spouses were very late home for their tea, especially in the weekends. The constable gave "Stocky" the ultimatum – "When the clock says twenty past six, I want to see the bar empty – is this understood?" Apparently all went well for a while but old habits die hard. One night around 8 p.m. "Stocky" had a good crowd in and in walked Constable Fowler.

"Tom," thundered the fully uniformed policeman, "What does the clock say?"

Tommy Stocktill straightened his shoulders, turned to the clock, then facing his questioner answered, "Tick tock, tick tock".

NINE WOMEN

Nine women came into the bar for a beer.
Nine women – was more than I'd seen in a year.
They were slender and shapely, blonde, brunette and red.
Out on safari, all basketball bred.

One barrel raced out on the rodeo ground.
She said she could ride fast and spin a horse round.
A drunken duckshooter flaked out in a chair
She casually emptied her drink in his ear.

He rose up as wild as a big grizzly bear
She ran back to her friends her heart full of fear.
He didn't know which one had done the dark deed
So he stumbled away in search of a feed.

One tried to take off an old cowboy's hat.
An old ex bull-rider – a good one at that –
He gave her the message – it caused her to frown –
Cowboys' hats are as sacred as a King's golden crown.

Some started to drink like they had lots of brass.
It was real costly stuff in a flash little glass.
When they left, the bartender, he started to curse,
One left with his glass stowed away in her purse.

One asked me so nicely to put down a verse.
So this is their story, for better or worse.
I'd rather have reached out and touched her soft hair –
Nine women came into the bar for a beer.

Blue Jeans, May '96
Ancient Briton, Naseby

Wicked Willy

In the '60s and '70s I spent a lot of my working life in Queenstown with Warren Cooper. What he did with his life from then on is well documented in the public arena but we did have some quiet private moments in this pub. The only other gathering place for the locals was the White Star, previously known as the Supreme Court Hotel. But this pub was special.

I rarely ever remember it being referred to by its correct name – McBrides – but most often it was called "Wicked's". The reason was simple. The proprietor was "Wicked Willy Cooper", perhaps one of Queenstown's most legendary characters who, with a few words would clear his bar of thirsty patrons if things weren't going well. But the clientele always came back and "Wicked" ruled for many years. Willy Cooper's diminutive, quietly spoken wife Cassie, was just the anchor Willy needed and woebetide anyone who criticised her man. "Lovee" the cook was almost as legendary as her employer, a lot quieter but what a meal she presented.

In 1883 Mrs McBride was the proprietress of McBrides Family Hotel on this same site. Her advertisement of the day proclaimed "all the comforts of a home can be had". Thinking back, I can't help but compare the small, warm bar and the matching lounge and dining room of "Wicked's" old pub in Beach Street with the large, shiny and sometimes brash hotels of present day Queenstown. It's really no contest!

Shingle Creek

In 1867 Patrick Galvin was the licensee of the very first hotel in this isolated part of Central Otago – halfway between Alexandra and Roxburgh on Highway 8. It has obviously been rebuilt but I couldn't resist drawing some of the buildings at the back of the present tavern. In this part of New Zealand you can almost bet on there being a relic or two of the past behind or even inside these country hotels simply because the dry climate has preserved these stone and sun-dried brick structures – no rust – no rot!

This Patrick Galvin was a real character who was born in County Clare, Ireland, in 1840 and went to Australia in 1857. He arrived in Otago about 1862 and by 1864 he had established the Sportsman's Arms in Alexandra, but a disgruntled Patrick gave up this licence in 1867 because he was not permitted to play music on the premises. This was particularly irksome for this Irishman who was a very accomplished Scottish and Irish piper. Next came Shingle Creek and that was followed by a residency, in 1904, at Cardrona which was by that time starting to run out of gold. Today a pleasant bar and dining room is at the disposal of the many tourists who travel this route all year round. It's a family venture run by Alister, Marilyn and Deanne Brown who are a very welcoming family.

Chatto Creek

"Good accommodation for the boarders and travellers. Best brands of wines and spirits kept in stock." This was the advertisement which D. G. Gunn used to entice trade to his Chatto Creek Hotel in 1902. This is a familiar story. Chatto Creek was a camping ground for the bullock wagons which plodded their creaking way across the dusty plains. The drivers shared the hotel which grew to care for the wants of the men employed on Moutere Station. I was talking to a friend in the racing industry recently who has made a regular pilgrimage to the Omakau races who remembers Ted Scott who ran this pub in the '60s.

It must be gratifying for the hosts of these establishments to have their regulars come back year after year, forming lasting friendships – something that doesn't happen so often in the city hotels. I made this drawing in 1996 shortly after Owen and Lesley Middlemass had taken over. When I went back in 2005 I was saddened to learn that Owen has passed away. Lesley is carrying on the business and I reflected on this as I had my lunch on the verandah in the warm, winter sun.

It take a special kind of courage and a special person to run an isolated country pub and it seemed to be running well during my visit, but don't forget to have a look at the brightly coloured mural in the "Gents" – it's signed by Helen Clark! In fact there are two signatures – one of the two belong to our Olympic hockey goalie and I'll leave it to you to work out the other. By the way, this work of art is not likely to be auctioned for charity.

The Albion at Luggate

In 1978 I stopped off here to make this drawing. In 2005 I went back and was greeted by Sean Colbourne, one of the owners of a pub that has changed considerably since my first visit. The mud plaster that was applied over the original stonework has been stripped off and the interior is a real treat complete with polished wood floors.

Like the old Parawa Hotel, this watering hole was regularly patronised by those amazing young men in their flying machines during the early days of top-dressing and deer shooting and recovery. Just up the road at Wanaka there is a vintage aircraft collection and its founder Sir Tim Wallis lived at the back of this hotel for two years in his early days of aviation pioneering. Around the walls are photos of the young pilots and their wartime planes who came home to fly helicopters, Tiger Moths, Fletchers and Harvards, at low levels over our farmlands and mountains after the war.

This hotel was built in 1867, a Mr Maidman being the original proprietor. Mr Trevathon was next in line and held possibly the longest tenancy, having spent 24 years (1881-1905) at this historic watering hole. Thomas Hopkins had two spells behind the bar from 1951-56 and again from 1959-62. Another host, familiar to me, was Brian McAuliffe who was a better than average player and coach of basketball and was present when I made my first drawing of the Albion.

Eichardt's Hotel

In 1891, each of the four Queenstown hotels were run by women. Eichardt's helm was held steady by Mrs Eichardt, McBrides Hotel by Mrs J. M. McBride, the Supreme Court Hotel (later the White Star) by Mrs O'Meara and the Mountaineer by Mrs R. Bond. I wonder if any other town in New Zealand can claim such a record.

Wakatipu Pioneer Gilbert Rees – a cousin of legendary cricketer W. G. Grace – once had a woolshed on this site which he demolished to build an hotel called the Queen's Arms. After bringing law and order to the Arrow diggings, Sergeant-Major Bracken resigned his police commission to enter a partnership with Gilbert Rees. Bracken was highly regarded by the miners in those rough and ready days in Arrowtown and so it seems he was similarly regarded as a publican as was his wife who held the licence. The hotel was then let to an ex-bank employee, T. H. Browne. The next owner was retired Prussian Army Officer, Captain Eichardt. He was known as a thoroughly nice chap who set about rebuilding this hotel in brick and stone. I have a special reason for remembering Eichardt's Hotel in the '70s, quite apart from the convivial times spent in the bar, because, along with bassist Bill Voight and local legend Lou Tombs on guitar and vocals, I played some hilarious gigs. I recall we played on the tiny stage at the end of the bar from 7 pm till 9 pm then we physically pushed, heaved and carried speaker boxes, guitars and a drum kit up the Mall to O'Connell's Cellar Bar where we played till late! Lou Tombs spent a lot of his daylight hours playing pool on the Eichardt's table with his constant opponent Dr Bruce Todd. Bruce only had to keep his eye on (between shots) the door of his surgery through the large front windows, to keep his patients in good health.

Roxburgh's Commercial

This grand old pub is so typical of the rather splendid buildings erected when towns like Roxburgh were in their infancy. It was established in 1866 and must have been the centre of attention whilst being built. Now, almost 140 years later it is still a reminder of days gone by – painted a pinkish red with white trim, it reminds me of a large wedding cake! This town had its beginnings where the gold was first found in 1862 on the east bank of the mighty Clutha River. Gradually as interest grew on the west bank, the prospectors drifted over and eventually settled on the present site of Roxburgh – named after an ancient ruined town on Scotland's Teviot River. When I arrived in the South Island in 1951 I watched the then massive Roxburgh Hydro Dam take shape. In 1955 the floodgates were closed and many sightseers swarmed downstream to try their prospecting skills on the beaches from which the river had receded, but they had little more luck than their predecessors.

Roxburgh's fame is now the annual glow of Autumn colours and the fresh fruit and vegetables that are produced from this fertile area. In 1883 there were five hotels in this town. Mr H. H. Heron held the licence for this hotel and the remaining four were Ormonds, Albion, the Queen's Head, and the inevitable Temperance. *The Benger Mail* was published each Wednesday and Mr J. Weatherall was the proprietor and I presume, the editor.

Another gent of the same name – W. Weatherall – was one of seven storekeepers, three of these being run by Chinese. Ah Hee, Chee Fung and Young Ho Kee were obviously left over from the gold prospecting era.

In 1936 an advertisement for this hotel told us that Thomas Blanchard was the proprietor and that "this fine establishment was under viceregal patronage."

The Governor General must have dropped in for a "cuppa" during his term of office . . .

The Royal Oak, Arrowtown

In 1890s this hotel was listed as the Royal Oak. Mr J. L. Jopp was the proprietor. Other hotels in this goldmining town were the Temperance, the New Orleans, the Ballarat and the Lake Hayes. As was usual in these rough and tumble times hotels were the refuge for the many who toiled hard in this unforgiving land. Then in 1936, for an unknown reason a Mr A. McPherson (late of the Club Hotel in Bluff) displayed a sign on the edge of the verandah proclaiming that this was the Central Hotel. He had the telephone connected (the post and telegraph office was next door) and the number was 2M, obviously on a party line!

He boasted a first class table, Speights ale on tap, superior accommodation and only the best brands of wines and spirits were stocked. One-and-a-half miles from the hotel was Lake Hayes where excellent fishing could be experienced and all this for the astounding tariff of eight shillings (80c). I made this drawing in about 1960 when the name had reverted back to the Royal Oak. Now sadly this little pub has disappeared under the developer's hammers – another link broken in the story of this historic town.

Welcome Home Inn, Skippers

Early in my married life I borrowed my mother-in-law's 1936 Dodge coup and headed off with my new wife to Queenstown and eventually Skippers. It has been recorded that of all the diggings in the Wakatipu, Skippers was the most rewarding to those hardy souls who made the journey to this remote spot.

In 1866, the journey alone must have been frightening enough without the thought of the back-breaking work of mining that lay ahead. Today it is no less frightening – winding, narrow without barriers and should only be attempted in a reliable motorcar and a driver with a reasonable degree of competence. However, to get back to my own story, it appears that the rather primitive (by today's standards) braking system in the old "Dodge" had decided to partially give up and for the return trip I had only a handbrake and a very low gear to assist me down to lake level. It's still difficult to describe my absolute fear during that journey and I can still remember the reaction of my wife when she was made aware of what had happened.

This little hotel must have provided some rest and relief to the many weary travellers in those far off days.

Beaumont Hotel

I first visited this hotel in 1976 when I stopped to draw the Beaumont Store which also served as post office and garage. The remains of this building still stand rather forlornly over the bridge from the pub. Now, only the hotel remains to tempt the traveller to stop for refreshments. If you've ever stopped at Raes Junction you will notice a similarity of design shared by the Beaumont and Junction Hotels. This is because they were both built, in the late '30s, by the same chap – a German who left his political philosophy behind in the form of a swastika design in the brickwork. They weren't left in an obvious place but in the case of the Beaumont building it was about 40cm square and placed at eye level in a back porch entrance. I'll bet that left a sour taste in the mouths of returning servicemen in 1945! The original hotel was of wooden construction, two-storeyed, complete with upper floor verandah and fancy railing. Like so many of the early wooden pubs it burned to the ground. Not many of these buildings were saved in those days because the best you could hope for was the bucket brigade manned by the locals. I had a pleasant chat and a cup of tea with mine host Gus Porter who seems ideally suited to the role of country pub host.

Clark's Junction

The original building was erected in about 1867 by a Mr Glens. He was followed by John Clark who gave the hotel and accommodation house its name which has survived. I've found during this odyssey that some of the hotels have had at least three name changes. The new proprietor was Alex McDonald who then sold it to Mr A. W. Stott. On 2 September 1932, fire destroyed the hotel but it was soon replaced with a modern (by standards of the day) new building. In writings of the day in 1869 it was described as "a small accommodation house kept by Mr Broadway" and it was noted by the writer that he "observed a man sitting on a case of whisky and gin with pannikins and corkscrew – that being all the wayfarers could find and indeed expect"! When you visit this wayside inn on Highway 87 make sure you examine a small collection of early photographs in the bar. Among them you will find a group standing outside this pub in the 1930s. At the extreme right you'll see "Arkwright" straight out of that wonderful TV series *Open All Hours*. The only thing missing the forlorn, long suffering "Granville" . . . that wonderful comedian Ronnie Barker will never be dead as long as this photo hangs in the Clarks Junction Hotel. If you can't find it ask Gillian or Min Bardwick – mine hosts for the past nine years and if you are wanting conversation, just ask this friendly couple about their golf handicaps – you'll be there for hours!

Dansey's Pass Hotel

This hotel, built in 1862, stands on the Maniototo side of this quite unique road between Duntroon in the Waitaki and the historic Kyeburn district. When I first drew this building in the late '50s it was of mainly schist rock construction. It is the most northern oasis on the Maniototo and aptly named (the English translation is "the plain of blood"). There were some very sad deaths recorded in its earliest days and at least one murder for which a Chinese miner was executed. However, the construction of the original pub was a story in itself. Like the original Stanley's Hotel at Macrae's Flat which the legendary "Budge" built for beer over a period of about five years, a fellow by the name of "Happy Bill" did similarly at Kyeburn. Bill's remuneration was also a daily diet of beer. The deal was that he was rewarded with a pint for every schist boulder, shaped and laid on the building site. On one particular occasion he had a very busy and productive rock laying day which resulted in a very happy evening for Bill. He apparently went on a walkabout and fell in to an open grave in the local cemetery in which he slept away what was left of the night. When he regained consciousness he really thought he had met his maker! But it was not enough for him to swear off the demon drink.

In 1869 Danseys Pass was known as "the insolvency court for citizens who found themselves in financial trouble". Hence the coined phrase, "through the pass or through the court". Edwin George owned the pub from 1863-76. Other proprietors through the years have been H. Forward from 1923-28, A. Loudon 1948-58, F. and M. Moynahan 1958-87 and E. R. and S. Carr since 1987. In 1870 the Kyeburn diggings had at least six unlicensed grog shanties and in 1880 there were 600 Chinese mining this harsh land.

Buckham's Brewery

No chronicle of southern pubs would be complete without mention of at least one brewery. The drawings throughout this book display the various well-known brands of beer but none of the pioneer ales such as the one manufactured in the early days by the Wakatipu Brewery and Cordial Company.

William Lovel Davis, an English brewer and Mr T. Surman, an American cordial maker, established the Wakatipu Company in 1870. William Davis had a daughter called Daisy who caught the eye of young Henry Charles Buckham who worked as a miner and as a part time employee in the brewery – they were married in 1905 and lived in Reefton where Henry mined the Waiuku.

On the death of Daisy's father in 1908 they returned to Queenstown where in 1909 they took over the business which once stood on about half a hectare in Queenstown Bay, now the site of a large hotel complex. In 1915 Henry introduced the Buckham name to the brewery which operated till 1915 but the manufacture of cordials continued for some years.

I made drawings of the original cottage and malthouse in the late '50s but this is the only drawing I retained. Sadly, one morning the near neighbours awoke to find that this history had disappeared under the tracks of the bulldozers. So much for progress . . .

Bannockburn

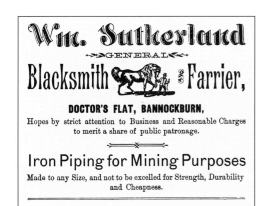

In 1891 there were three hotels in this busy settlement. Gold was discovered in the early 1860s and the accompanying "fever" continued for the next decade, and the Bannockburn, the Peaksville and the Reefers Arms no doubt did a brisk trade. In 1900 Donald McRae was the licensee of the Bannockburn Hotel which, apart from a small wooden facade, was barely more than a large corrugated iron shed. I presume this present day bar and restaurant stands on the original site but it's a far cry from its predecessor 105 years ago.

While compiling this book I often tried to imagine what sights a busy bar in a gold town would present to a thirsty traveller 100 years ago. Plenty of noise accompanying the drinking and smoking with perhaps an accordion and violin completing the scene. But there seemed to be a certain restraining influence in the form of the Christian church, because, according to my records there were at least four men of the cloth who visited this rough and tough outpost on a regular basis.

The Rev. F. W. Martin was the Episcopalian minister, along with the Rev. G. Hunter, Presbyterian; Rev. Fr McGrath Catholic and the Rev. Lanyon, Christian Brothers. They certainly weren't short of spiritual guidance!

Shotover Ferry Bridge Hotel

This is what this pub looked like when I first visited it in the mid '50s. It was originally known as the Shotover Ferry Bridge Hotel and in 1891 it was run by Sarah O'Kane. It has a special place in my memory bank because of a significant New Year's Eve in the early '60s. I was then working in a dance band and we were booked to bring in the New Year in the Shotover Hall which was just across the road from the pub.

Of course in those days the bars closed at 6 o'clock and the illicit comings and goings between the hall and the bar were frequent, particularly between dances. I also remember packing up and driving back to Invercargill at some unearthly hour of the morning, thinking that the only real winner was the publican who was lucky enough not to be visited by the local constabulary.

From memory there was just one policeman in Queenstown in those days in the form of Keith Munro. My how it has changed in 35 years from clustering around the boot of a car outside the dance hall (a punishable offence) to drinking in comfort in entertainment areas . . . in those days I couldn't quite make out what was the greatest evil, the dancing or the drinking or the combination of both.

The White Star

When I worked in Queenstown in the '60s and '70s this was the locals' bar run by the Midgley Family. The town was just beginning its growing pains and the tourists were filling the other watering holes such as McBrides, known affectionately as "Wicked Willys", the Mountaineer, run by the Brun family and Eichardts, none of which are serving ale to the locals these days. In the late 1800s this hotel traded under the rather grand name of the Supreme Court Hotel because, I suppose, it stood opposite the stone courthouse. The last memory I have of this old pub is of standing at the doorway of the bar watching John Hore-Grennell and his new bride drive past in a beautifully turned out horse and buggy. Like so many of these structures with a high timber content, it burned down in a spectacular fashion that many residents still remember. The area is now one of the few green recreational spots in an otherwise overcrowded central business district.

Dunstan Hotel

Benjamin Naylor owned this hotel in the late 1800s and Mr B. Murray was the manager. So read the advertisement in the Goldfield's Directory of 1891. The advertisement proudly proclaimed that the hotel was under the distinguished patronage of Sir George Grey, Sir George Bowen and Sir James Ferguson who, I presume, was of the same family of a later Governor General Sir Bernard Ferguson. The hotel was the terminus for Cobb and Co.'s coaches which travelled to Queenstown via Palmerston and Lawrence, these vehicles, no doubt being the mode of transport of these distinguished persons. It's interesting to note that one of Clyde's most notable residents, Jean Desiré Feraud, who mined for gold in the area used his water race to irrigate his property named "Monte Christo" on which he grew apricots, peaches and grapes. He sold his wines as far away as Dunedin, much to the astonishment of those who considered the soil of Central Otago as dry and useless!

Jean Desiré Feraud would no doubt have his faith in the soil justified, if he was able to see the wine revolution that has taken over this part of New Zealand. By the way – they thought that wine pioneer Alan Brady was a little crazy too!

Cardrona

In 1954 I drove for what seemed like hours from Wanaka to reach this hotel. The gravel road was fairly typical of the roads around this district at the time which was making its first serious moves towards establishing what is now a very crowded tourist mecca. On finding the bar unattended I wandered out the back to be confronted by a stern, bald, spectacled man wearing a collarless shirt and braces. We exchanged pleasantries and among the subjects was the Boer War in which he had fought. His rather forbidding demeanor softened when I shared with him the fact that my paternal grandfather had also participated in that war far away from New Zealand.

Jim Paterson took over the licence in 1926 and he reigned supreme till 1961 when he was aged 90! The licence then lapsed until in recent times this famous facade was restored, along with the licence. In 1883 there was one hotel at Cardrona – the All Nations, the licence being held by Joseph La Franchi, Paterson's future father-in-law. Then, in 1891 two hotels were listed in the local business directory, the other being the Cardona run by Mr J. Willoughby who it appears was also the blacksmith and storekeeper. Jim Paterson was born in 1871 and died in 1962 aged 91. He is buried in the tiny lower Cardrona cemetery beside his wife Ettie (née La Franchi).

The Railway Hotel at Ida Valley

In the mid '70s on a burning, bright Maniototo day I called at this oasis after finishing a drawing of the old schoolhouse down the road. Earlier, I had been drawing the Hayes engineering buildings eight kilometres away at Oturehua. I was told that at Ida Valley there was a pub, railway station and a school so I set off to make some drawings of a remote spot I knew nothing about. Well, remote it might be but it was pure sun-baked Maniototo!

From 1969 till 1991 I contributed a weekly feature for *The Southland Times* – a drawing and a story – so for those eventful 22 years I did a lot of travelling seeking out the elusive and sometimes quirky buildings, people and landscapes in New Zealand and overseas. In 1876 the Anderson family arrived in Otago from the Orkney Islands. Thomas Anderson had a son named William who bought "Hazel Hills", a large run in the Ida Valley in 1919. He married Mary Healy whose parents were the proprietors of this hotel which was established in 1902. Pubs seemed to run in this family as William's daughter Patricia and her husband Harry Perkins ran Perkins Family Hotel in Omakau, now long closed.

Ida Valley was the railhead for the Otago Central Branch Railway which closed in 1990. The old rail line is now a cycling, walking and horse trekking trail and on the day I made this drawing there seemed to be cyclists everywhere taking advantage of the early Autumn weather to explore this wonderful corner of our country. I met one of the owners of this wonderful link with our past, Chris Doudney, an architect at Otago University. He was busy tidying up the grounds in front of the pub which I can remember sporting a gravel drive. As well there are things going on inside and I was invited in to relive my first visit 36 years before.

Thank goodness for another historic building saved.

Oturehua Tavern

This pub was established by James Caldwell in 1899 who had previously been mine host at Wedderburn. Oturehua was originally known as Rough Ridge. This is the site of the original Rough Ridge Railway Hotel which Caldwell built to coincide with the arrival of the railway in 1900. This area is where the Hayes Family established their nationally famous engineering works in 1895. They are famous for their contribution to the farmers of the district in the form of the Hayes wire strainers and those famous windmills. Previous publicans to serve the thirsty locals and travellers have been Elizabeth and Arthur Islip in 1903 and in 1907 Michael and Mary Doy took over. Henry Allen in 1933 and in 1949 William Cook was mine host.

In the middle of each winter many hundreds of slightly mad motor cyclists arrive in this area to take part in the annual "Brass Monkey" rally where in zero and below temperatures they camp out and swap yarns and drink Speights for a weekend. This old hotel caters for many robust appetites and of course pull a few pints.

Post Office, Chatto Creek

In the course of my ramblings around Otago and Southland during the past 50 years, I've found some strange little post offices occasionally tucked away back in the corner of the local general store, or in the case of Parawa, standing almost alone in a green Southland pasture. That particular little post office was about the size of what used to be called a "single man's hut" and would be one of the few that could be reached by opening a farm gate and driving across a paddock which was just over the road from the Parawa Pub. Going to collect the mail was a good excuse to get away from the farm to sink a few Speights!

When the demolition of our rural services began in the '80s, among the first victims were those sturdy, sometimes ornate post offices. Luckily, most of them are still standing, being occupied for a number of reasons. Balclutha, Ophir, Winton, Riverton, Wyndham and Gore to mention just a few, stand proudly as monuments to the past when our lives ran just a little slower.

This quaint survivor stands beside the Chatto Creek Hotel and from 1933 till 31 January 1975 Mary-Rose Kinney reigned supreme as the post mistress. Luckily it hasn't been pushed over to make room for a bigger beer garden.

The Pub at Poolburn

There is a sign on the front of this hotel which proclaims that it is, "The meeting place of the valley". When you stand outside the front door and look around, you immediately wonder where all the people are that might meet at this well-appointed watering hole. The original hotel was further up the hill.

In the early '70s I made my first drawing of this present hotel. Outside the original front door stood a concrete mixer beside a pile of gravel which I included in the picture, not knowing how significant this was in the scheme of things until I learned more of the life and times of Bill O'Connor. Bill built this pub with lots of stops and starts, finally completing it in 1928. Bill was a big Irish-Australian blacksmith with a fiery temper. Many times during the long building process, fierce arguments would break out among his workers resulting in him sacking them all. They would all get on the booze, make up, and eventually resume building this hotel in the middle of nowhere. Bill was born in 1887 and died in 1939 aged 52. He was three times married – his first two wives pre-deceasing him. His third wife, Sarah Franklin, arrived in Poolburn as the result of an advertisement Bill placed in the Lawrence Newspaper Tuapeka Times. Bill wanted a music teacher for his daughter Monica. Sarah duly arrived and one can only imagine her immediate thoughts of first seeing this isolated hotel. However Bill's charm soon won this young lady over and they were duly married. They had four children – Pat, Maureen, Bill and Tom. Tom became mine host of the Mossburn Hotel after resigning from the police force in 1973.

The day I arrived to make this drawing was a fine, warm, calm Maniototo day and as I had made my way through this amazing country I was met at almost every turn by cyclists of all shapes, sizes and ages experiencing the adventure of the old rail trails that snake through this sun-burned land. Eventually they caught up with me at this pub but I did get an odd hour with the new owners, Chris and Sue Forrest who had not long before arrived from Amberley where Chris was a curbing contractor.

I'm sure these young folk will fit in to this community which is now beginning to reap the rewards of a new type of tourism.

The Kingston Connection

There are still a few railway hotels in areas where the giant steaming beasts of yesteryear huffed, puffed and clanked through towns and villages in the south. Some of the buildings have been spared.

Memorials such as platforms and waiting rooms, goods sheds and those wonderful, wooden, elevated water tanks that bear testimony to the skill of the cooper. This drawing of the Kingston Tavern was done in 1984 just prior to it burning down on 16 February. Only one of the many hotels (at least 10 of them) that have plied their trade at Kingston since 1863 have been named Railway even though Kingston was a railway terminus. Other hotels in this tiny settlement at the southern end of Lake Wakatipu have been the Post Office, the Exchange, the Criterion, the Royal Mail, the Lake Wakatipu, the Terminus and others, all trading between 1863 and 1890.

Kingston must have been quite a place to be when the train met the s.s. *Earnslaw* or paddle steamer *Mountaineer.* I can recall when tourists could travel by train from Dunedin or Invercargill to Kingston and board the *Earnslaw* to Queenstown. Perhaps we may see this old world excursion re-invented one day for the increasing number of tourists we are attracting these days.

Riversdale's Local

This weatherboard pub, standing on a main street corner could be almost anywhere in New Zealand. Only the people of Riversdale would recognise this little corner of their hamlet. In the space of a few hundred paces you could leave the police station, buy some groceries, have a bet at the TAB, leave the ute at the garage for a service, and have a few brown ales while watching the cricket on the telly in the bar. I find much quiet pleasure working in and around Southland's service towns. A few of the services have gone but these little towns have battled back from the adversity of the '80s and rural Southland is in good shape. This settlement was once the centrepiece of the New Zealand Agricultural Company – formed in 1878 – which amalgamated most of the properties between Gore and Lumsden. The recently built railway ensured that this area was accessible and busy in boom times. Now giant road transporters carry everything and keep the district council road contractors busy . . .

The Shamrock at Fairfax

I drove in from Isla Bank, across the Aparima River and there it was – the Shamrock, the Fairfax local. I've lived in the south long enough to remember that to get to the pub along this road I had to cross the railway line which was a busy line in the '50s. Now, only intermittent coal trains pass through on their way from Ohai to Invercargill.

In 1891 the Fairfax blacksmith was Mr W. Reidie, the manager of the dairy factory was J. McKinnon and Jim Sutherland was both postmaster and storekeeper but perhaps the glue that held this tiny village together was the Shamrock Hotel run by Mrs C. Callaghan.

It's not surprising that this was the only establishment that survived well into the 20th century. When the licence was lost it was inhabited by a family or two but finally it became dangerous and was demolished.

The first time I ever set foot in this pub was in the early '60s when I was attending a party at local farmer Roger Jackman's place. During the night someone suggested that we pop off down to the Shamrock and pick up Gill Dech. This famous pianist often spent long spells at the hotel where he could imbibe to his heart's content away from the public eye. Older readers will remember Gill's recording of *The Robin's Return*. It was one of the biggest-selling records ever in New Zealand.

Our party lasted till dawn and I well remember Gill Dech was still playing when I left – with memories of a great pub, legendary pianist and a marathon celebration.

Taylor's Creek Hotel

In about 1870 this hotel was built by Laughlan McKenzie where the road meets Taylor's Creek. His wife was apparently a great cook and it became a meeting place for prospectors, shepherds, shearers and runholders alike. The licence was lost and by 1906 the building alone remained as a reminder of the past. Taylor's Creek is in the Wairaki Station area of Blackmount and when I came to Southland the road through Blackmount to Manapouri and Te Anau was a very primitive one compared to the highway known as the Southern Scenic Tourist Route today. The researching of this pub turned up more than I first expected. While reading the *75th School and Community Jubilee Book* by Moira Pelvin, I noticed a reference to F. W. Aylmer who was a runholder on Wairaki Station in 1863. His wife died shortly after she arrived at Wairaki and is buried on the property but her husband died of dropsy in 1867 and is buried in the East Road Cemetery in Invercargill.

I will now attempt to explain why I was interested in these people.

In 1969 I found (by accident) the grave and headstone of the son of General H. W. Gordon, Royal Artillery, and brother of General C. G. Gordon of Khartoum. William A. Gordon the older brother of the hero of Khartoum came to New Zealand in about 1863 and was employed as a tutor to the children of F. William Aylmer, the Wairaki Station runholder. I now fast forward to 2002 when I was writing and illustrating a book of Invercargill homes and people when I went back out to the city cemetery to check on W. A. Gordon's headstone, only to find that it had completely disappeared!

Luckily the cemetery administrators still have the names, dates and plot numbers on their computer but I have the only known image of that gravestone. I might add that the staff were mystified as to how they could lose a large headstone and concrete slab. All that stands in that space are a few shrubs – better than nothing I suppose . . .

The Criterion at Round Hill

In 1888 the Round Hill Goldfield had probably the largest Chinatown in New Zealand. Gold was first found here by two Italians with the unlikely names of Leecy and Mitchell but they couldn't make their claim pay so off to nearby Riverton they went to make their living fishing as the locals do to this day. Other Europeans didn't persist so in moved the hard working, meticulous Chinese and "Canton" was born along with this hotel. The Te Hun Fong Hotel was kept by Ly Chong. Apparently it was as neat and clean as a new pin considering the disreputable, rundown appearance of the rest of the township.

Ly was a good humoured man always ready to attend to his patron's every wish. In 1893 the Rev. Alexander Don, missioner to the Chinese mining community, revisited Round Hill and "found it much changed". From a population of around 400 it had diminished to 140. Ly Chong's hotel had been sold to a succession of Europeans, among them the Hanning family but bad luck was in store for this once fine hotel. In 1924 the building was shifted by placing logs beneath it and hauling it a short distance with a seven horse power traction engine. Considering it weighed 46 tons this was quite a feat. It took four days to shift it to its new location and it was back in operation – complete with billiard room – in three weeks. Alas, six years later it burned to the ground on Friday, 17 June 1938 at 4 o'clock in the morning.

Commercial Tavern, Wairio

During my early years in Southland I ventured off the main road to Nightcaps one day and found some interesting old wooden stable buildings, resplendent in their barn-red paint, just faded enough to be of interest to an artist. I always promised myself that I would return to make drawings of the railway offices and the pub.

Well, I finally made it and here I present the local tavern. The building is not architecturally challenging but the history around this railway settlement deserves recording. The village was surveyed by Henry E. Moors in 1880 as the terminus for the N.Z. Railways line from Invercargill via Thornbury and Otautau which was officially opened on 3 March 1882. To mark the occasion a train carrying 300 passengers travelled from Invercargill to this tiny village. As I sat outside the pub I tried to imagine the scene of these visitors in their finery milling around the area between the hotel and the railway station. It was probably one of the best days trading the publican Mrs Price and Mr Baird the storekeeper had experienced in a while. In 1905, just a century ago the township consisted of a Presbyterian church, public hall, hotel and general store which also housed the post and telegraph offices. Today, the railway, the hall, the church and the pub remain but of course the manpower that ran the trains and the post office in those days have long since been made redundant by a succession of political experiments and technology but somehow Wairio has survived despite it all, justifying mine hosts, Marlene and Craig Burgess, keeping a welcome ready for the locals and the thirsty traveller.

HOKONUI MOONSHINE

Lynley Dear

When you're stilling, lie low, for stilling is slow,
you crouch by your still out of sight.
Watch over your stash of the good barley mash,
in the braw amber light of a Moonshine-y night.

It was out at Hokonui, north-west the plains of Gore,
that the "Chief" by name of big Murdoch McRae
brewed the whisky that was good,
malt maturing in the wood,
"Hokonui", famous to this very day.

It was tasted near and far, you could buy it in the jar
or even in the milkman's jerry can.
Had the tangy taste of peat
from the waters of Duck Creek,
"Hokonui", famous where a man's a man.

When you're stilling, lie low, for stilling is slow,
you crouch by your still out of sight.
Watch over your stash of the good barley mash
in the braw amber light of a Moonshine-y night.

From Dunsdale and from Hedgehope and round by Timpany's
came the fiery glow that flamed across your chest.
Should be four years in the cask
but they couldn't make it last
and pronounced it better than auld Scotland's best.

Famous not just in the sticks, for as late as "46"
you could quaff it back and feel that mellow bite.
Could be sampled (nudge and wink)
where the Government laddies drink
in the braw amber glow of a Wellington night.

When you're stilling, lie low, for stilling is slow,
and the police could come by on his horse
The law's on his side
and his breeches gleam white
in the braw amber light of a Moonshine-y night.

The Hokonui Distiller

Long ago I was asked to draw an illegal whisky still. I can't remember why but I do remember approaching the local police photographer in the hope that he may have in his collection a photo of a still they had found and photographed for evidence. The copper was an amiable fellow who helped me to reconstruct a typical still. Of course the chap in the bowler hat wasn't in the photo but he does appear to be anxiously waiting for something "spiritual" to happen. And as this book is about hotels and the characters who supped the merchandise, I thought a product as southern as "Hokonui Moonshine" was too important to overlook.

Thornbury Tavern

In the days when the pubs closed at 6 pm and it was difficult to buy a packet of fags and a loaf of bread after 5 pm, this was a great place to shop for the Sunday beer – just a short drive from Invercargill or Riverton and if you knew the ropes – relatively easy. My, how those licensing laws have changed our culture. Some say for the worse.

In 1891 Mr R. Foster was not only the host of the Junction Hotel at Thornbury but was a merchant with Wittingham and Instone and if that wasn't enough, he ran the railway refreshment rooms. But wait, there's more! According to Mills and Dick's Business Directory of 1891 he was listed as a storekeeper.

The station master was Mr T. F. Roskruge and Mr A. Weir was the blacksmith and wheelwright. Licensees through the years have included Rob and Paula Dixon, Ken and Noeline Hamlin, and names such as Turner, Drake, Hannah, Tisdale, Williams and Wybrow are still remembered around the district. When the railway line ran through this village there was a saddler, bootmaker, blacksmith, a mercantile firm, storekeeper, wheelwright and a post office.

Those are gone but between Colac Bay and this pub (a distance of about 20km) there are seven hotels! What does that say about our priorities? There is something very special about our country pubs. A culture that doesn't present any feeling of unease that is often sensed in city hotels. Let's stay loyal to these places of recreation so that they remain part of our wonderful rural lifestyle.

Mine Hostess – Peg Taylor

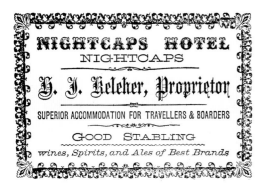

My abiding memory of Peg and her hotel at Ohai was a table, groaning under the weight of home-baked cakes, biscuits and mountains of sandwiches. It's mid afternoon and John Gordon of "A Dog's Show" fame and a TVNZ crew are filming Peg and the pub for a series called "The Southlanders". It was first seen, in six one-hour episodes, in 1981 and was so popular that the complete series was replayed a year later. Peg Taylor was renowned for her "table" at the hotel and as well for her contributions when someone in the village had to cope with a bereavement – it was called "bake and take". Peg was born in Nightcaps in 1899 and even though she was known all over New Zealand as a successful publican she never took an alcoholic drink in her life!

In 1951 Ohai was granted a licence to build an hotel. Up until this time the miners had to trek to Nightcaps for their tipple. If they didn't have any transport they caught a coal truck which were back and forth all day. The Nightcaps Hotel was once known as the "Miner's Rest" and after a journey on push bike or coal truck, a rest is certainly what was wanted and it must be remembered that in the '50s, few people owned a car.

Lumsden's Royal Mail Hotel

I used to stay overnight in Lumsden quite often in my early days in Southland – the days when a lot of the roads from Dunedin and Invercargill that led to the lakes were a mixture of narrow tar seal and gravel and a break was welcome. I usually stayed with the legendary Nelson Crosbie and his wife across the road from this classic.

In 1883 there were four hotels at the Elbow (as Lumsden was known then) – the Elbow operated by Mr H. Howells, Joseph Crosbie's Waimea, G. Tucker's Royal Mail and the Castlerock operated by G. Beer.

By 1891 the hotels were down to three – considering the small population of these early towns it's a wonder they lasted as long as they did, but the Elbow, the Railway and the Royal Mail survived in to the 20th century when the steam trains were in full swing. In those days Queenstown could be reached by rail and steamer and the accommodation aspect of these pubs was as important as the bar trade.

On 24 May 2005, after 15 years, publicans Lorraine and Brian Chamberlain closed the doors. Smoking bans and drink driving risks took its toll on the bar trade and the many fishermen and women from here and abroad missed the hospitality of Brian and Lorraine. During their tenure they not only housed and fed their patrons but also catered for the local maternity home, meals on wheels and daycare meals for the elderly.

Then along came a young couple by the name of Tony and Alison Cleland who have transformed this historic hotel. It is now a building to be proud of. After a complete restoration inside and out it now houses a restaurant, accommodation and conference facilities.

Parawa Junction

This hotel holds very special memories for me, as it does for many others, particularly during the years from 1961 to 1968 when that delightful couple, Peg and John Newman, were the proprietors. When John was invalided out of the navy in 1942 he was told that his "number was up" as he had contracted tuberculosis, so it was back to New Zealand and the Waipiata Sanitorium.

I recently spent an afternoon with this couple at their retirement home in Arrowtown and there was a great deal of reminiscing. John told me that he decided that the TB was not going to claim him so he departed the sanitorium and embarked on a 12 year career as mine host of the Kingston Hotel from 1944-48, Parawa Junction Hotel from 1961-68 and the Garston Hotel from 1968-69. At one stage John ran the Parawa operation while Peg managed the Garston. What a busy couple and now into their 80s they are still laughing about the great times and the fascinating people they hosted.

Parawa Junction was named thus, when this tiny pub was virtually at the junction of the main highway to Queenstown and the road to Nokomai. Hordes of fishers have, over the years, told tall tales and drunk tall ales in the Parawa bar after fishing the Nokomai. Forestry and DOC staff had many meetings and made decisions in John and Peg's bar and regular visits by Southland's pioneer aviators were commonplace. Bill Black, Ron Bush and Bill Hewitt are just three of the characters who literally dropped in on the Newmans, thanks to a large paddock at the rear of the hotel.

In the '60s, a dance band I was a part of made regular trips to Queenstown and a stop at the Parawa was compulsory. Often on the long hungover trip home, we stopped here to refresh ourselves and generally the lid of the piano was lifted and the party began. Recently, Pat Soper, *Southland Times* feature writer and one time Parawa pantry-maid, told me that the old piano is still there!

There have been 15 licensees in this hotel since its beginnings in the early 1860s, among them being John Bush who passed on the baton in 1870 to John Gibson. Percy Challis followed his brother Alf late in the 19th century followed by a Dr Moorhouse.

I have no idea what he was a doctor of, but he and Tom Shirley catered for the tired and thirsty travellers until 1914. The pub seemed to change hands on a fairly regular basis until John and Peg Newman came in May 1961 and finally closed the doors in September 1968.

All Alone at Benmore

During my 50 years of living in Southland I've made many hundreds of trips north past this hotel. It reminds me of those rather lonely rural war memorials which stand totally alone. The only reference to the location in which it stands are the names and district in which the soldiers lived and worked.

The sign on the pub is the only mention of the name of the district as far as I can find. The area was also known as "Harringtons". In 1866 Queen Victoria granted Hugh McLean title to the land and permission to build an hotel. Those were the days when what passed for a road was busy with coaches, bullock wagons and those on foot on their way to the goldfields. Dipton and Centre Bush were north and south of this pub as was the case in those pioneering days when the food, drink and stabling were a day's walk apart or about 20 miles.

An Honours Board in this bright little bar tells us who has held the licence and included are John Morrison in 1870, Frederick Benson in 1874, Donald McMillan in 1891, William Bryce in 1915 and Susan Barker McLean (widow) 1934. I wonder if she was of the same family of McLean the founder?

In the 1936 *Motorists Road Guide* she advertised the fact that she served only the best wines and spirits, morning and afternoon teas and good accommodation. She is pictured standing under the verandah of the original hotel which was built behind this present building. It looked more like a general store, unlike the 1936 art deco hotel of today.

Romanian born Diana (pronounced Deanna) and John McDougall met each other on the internet and are now the proud owners of the Benmore. Diana's welcoming smile enhances her warm European accent. It was good to experience some real old world charm.

The Garston Hotel

Two large sheep stations, Greenvale and Glenquoich, virtually established the district we know as Garston – the farthest inland settlement in New Zealand. The first hotel was run by W. D. Soper built of stone and established in 1876. Garston became recognised as a settlement about 1858. Gold was discovered in 1862 and many of the miners gave up when the gold gave out and there began the farms they moved on to after the land was surveyed into blocks in 1876.

W. D. Soper's stone pub was replaced in 1912 by a large two-storeyed wooden building but this, like a lot of the original wooden hotels, burned down in 1935. This hotel, with a touch of art deco, was built in 1939. Next to and to the north of the present pub there are the remains of the original stables which, I note, have had some preservation work done on them. They date back to the 1870s. I first became acquainted with this pub and its accommodation when mine hosts were Peg and Cam Murdoch. Cam's brother ran his garage from the stables. Now years later, a modern garage and petrol pumps operate from across the road.

A feature of Garston that I've always admired is the neatly kept terrace area over the road from the hotel where once perched the post and telegraph office and those two, tiny, immaculately kept wooden churches which are still in use. This completes a tiny village which once boasted a ski field and a skating rink.

Chub's Bar in Winton

This category two historic place replaced the original Railway Hotel which burned down in 1909. The building was completed in 1910 by the man responsible for building the original railway line from Invercargill.

In 1883 Mr F. R. White was the proprietor and Winton's Mayor was Mr C. D. Moore. In 1891 Mr G. M. Starkey had taken over and Constable Mulholland was keeping law and order in the town. In 1991, John and Nancy McHugh bought the brewery-owned hotel and set about bringing it up to a high standard, both in catering and accommodation. John is involved in the community board as its present chairman. He is past president of the local Lion's Club, the Rugby Club and the RSA Bowling Club; just a few of his local involvements.

In the public bar there hangs an Honours Board naming the publicans and policemen from the earliest days of the pub's history. For instance, in 1862, it states that "Sergeant Morton and several constables kept law and order", not very specific but perhaps the lower ranks didn't warrant individual mention in those days.

In 1934 Constable William Cooper took over only to lose his life later during the Stanley Graham siege on the West Coast of the South Island. Another well-known character was Constable Brian "Gibby" Gibson – a keeper of the peace from 1971. A highlight of this pub's history was the day that Sir Anthony Hopkins and the film crew arrived to shoot a sequence of *The World's Fastest Indian* in and around the pub and the bank next door. John and Nancy have fond memories of that very amiable gentleman – Sir Anthony Hopkins.

The Waiau Tavern

In 1910 this licence was located across the mighty Waiau River where the local dairy factory once operated. The first licensee was Mr Walker.

After being burned down the Waiau was relocated to its present site on Tuatapere's main road. After 20 years the recently retired licensees Pam and David McNay called it a day in 2003 – they moved to their home in Arrowtown but the ever-busy Dave is still organising things like the annual Stewart Island Fishing Competition which has attracted celebrity fishers from all over the country and beyond for years.

Dave has been a trustee of the Borland Lodge, the home of the Southland Youth Adventure Trust, president and founding member of the Hump Track High Country Adventure as well as being a vice president and life member of the Hotel Association of New Zealand. His involvement in the local Tuatapere Squash, Bowling and Rugby Clubs points up the importance of a community spirit in these small towns in Otago and Southland.

The Royal, Waikaka

The discovery of gold in 1867 was the reason for this pleasant little settlement coming into existence. Donald McKenzie was the first to discover the elusive metal about three miles from the township. Water was perhaps the most important ingredient in the process of winning the gold from the ground and water races were dug (mainly by hand) from the Waikaka River to a distance of nine miles. Imagine the effort needed to carry out such a task. They were certainly hardy souls . . . In 1871 there were an estimated 200 Chinese and 90 Europeans working the claims. According to writings in 1873 "It is estimated that there are now 300 white men and 500 yellow men digging and searching for gold". Imagine writing in that style in these excessively PC days!

In 1873 the town was shifted from the diggings to this present site. There were two hotels – the Star owned by Hunter and Adamson and the original Royal by Mr W. Edge. Today the town boasts a store, postal centre, two garages, a civic centre, a fine lodge building, a Scout hall, playcentre and a couple of churches. But the social hub of the village is the Royal Hotel run by Louise and Jack Meehan. The building dates back to 1887.

On the day I made this drawing there was a busload of elderly folk in the hotel lounge enjoying a game of housie. It was mid afternoon and I thought "How much more rural New Zealand could this be?" In earlier times, from 1908-62, excursions such as these may have been made by railway. Perhaps not to play housie but a WDFF meeting methinks. Sadly most of the branch lines of the rail system have gone with only a few signs of the tracks showing through in the well-grassed paddocks.

The Winton Hotel

In the 1890s the licensee of this proud-looking hotel was Mr C. D. Moore who was also the town's mayor and baker! The town was established in 1861 and was named after Thomas Winton. In 1863 Great North Road was cut from the dense native bush as the town was rapidly becoming an important stop for those optimistic souls enroute to the goldfields. Winton is believed to be the oldest inland town in Southland. Among the many publicans to inhabit this historic pub are the current hosts Karen and Russell Drake, Diane and Blair Bayne, the legendary Ivan West (of White House fame) and ex-All Black Leicester Rutledge, whose family is still involved with rugby at provincial level.

The Commercial, Mossburn

In the 1890s Mossburn had two hotels – the Commercial, run by James Dore (a name still known in the area) and George Beer's Junction. By 1936 the Commercial was the sole "watering hole" in the district as is the case these days. In the '30s this hotel was run by another well-known name in transport and hospitality – (Frank) F. J. Crosbie. In the late 1890s the railway was the lifeline and it's interesting to note that the Mossburn Railway Station was looked after by a caretaker by the name of Mrs McNeil. Nothing as grand as a stationmaster with peaked hat and shiny buttons that we remember so fondly. But to make up for that the village had two Justices of the Peace! Mr A. Browning and a name that came to be associated with a type of pasture grass and in a later generation, politics. His name was George Chewings of "Chewings Fescue" fame. Another publican who presided over the local "flock" was ex-policeman Tom O'Connor who eventually moved to Invercargill to manage the Don Lodge and latterly the Newfield Tavern for the Invercargill Licensing Trust. Tom's interests include boxing at local and national level and by all accounts was himself a more than handy boxer. After 16½ years in the police force Tom O'Connor took his wife Lewin and their children, Stephen, Christine and Shelley, to Mossburn to start a new life as the lessee of the Railway Hotel. That was Easter 1975. Like most country pubs it had its share of local identities. Among them was a fellow known as "Encyclopaedia" – "Fiddle" Hair, an entertainer in his own right who was always accompanied by his faithful dog "Oscar". He was a large man with a sense of humour to match and was easily recognisable in his Mark I Zephyr which was never in danger of receiving a speeding ticket and was well-known for stopping in the middle of the road. Creatures of habit are often attached to country pubs. One such was Tom Gallagher – a lovely man of few words. His visits to the pub were more regular than clockwork! He would arrive every morning at precisely 11.10 am and then again at 4.20 pm. He would have two or three half pints then depart. The barman would pull his half pint at those exact times each day and place them at the railway end of the bar. Without fail he would arrive quietly, quaff his ale and depart without ceremony. On the very rare occasions that he didn't appear, local enquiries were immediately made as to his whereabouts and health – the sign of a truly caring society.

During the days of 6 o'clock closing, there wasn't a country pub that wasn't visited by the law who, thanks to the telephone and keen-eyed locals, usually found an empty, smoky bar and a full car park. This happened once when Tom O'Connor was away in Australia. His wife Lewin was running the bar when a police patrol car was spotted nearby. She cleared the bar and emptied the patrons into the hotel flat, when in strode the legendary Sergeant Warwick Maloney from Queenstown. Whether he believed that mine hostess was having a private party was not revealed by this no-nonsense sergeant as he politely wished Lewin a very good night and departed . . . Tom shared with me the fact that "the smoke in the bar was so thick you needed a search warrant to find your way"!

The Aparima Hotel

The land on which this hotel stands was originally granted to one Samuel Hodgkinson by the Crown in 1866. His wife, Mary Eliza was issued a Certificate of Title in 1872 and it was transferred in March 1874 to Matthew Instone, a merchant of Riverton, who then subdivided it into five lots in 1878. Then along came Frederick Joseph Locke who purchased Lot 5 for the princely sum of £325 ($650). This area was known as the "Township of Trentham" and after building the pub, Joseph was mine host until at least 1899.

In 1946 an engine driver by the name of John Batchelor and a farmer, Francis Batchelor – obviously related – ran the hotel until Joseph Hilderbrand from Colac Bay took over in 1951. The following year Joseph sold out to Alan Inglis who remained behind the bar until 1964. This is about the time that I first became familiar with this hotel – particularly on the odd occasion when my musical colleague Bill McLachlan and I took a tincture or two after six o'clock. Weren't they exciting times! When I moved to Riverton in the late '80s mine host and hostess were Margaret and Ernie Brown who have since retired to live the good life on a hill overlooking beautiful Taramea Bay.

Orepuki

When the railway came to this little town in 1885 it boasted a population of more than 3,000! Passing through this hamlet today you would find this statistic hard to believe but in those far off days there was a very good reason – in fact, several good reasons such as gold, shale, iron and platinum. In 1879 the New Zealand Coal and Oil Company was formed in London with a capital of £180,000 ($360,000). This was a vast amount of money in those times and it was poured into the gigantic shale works erected in the district. Adam (Addie) Adamson was the mayor of Invercargill from 1953 to 1962 and his first job was in the office of the shale works. Later he ran a general store in Orepuki. In 1902 the works closed abruptly amid rumours of a suspicious nature.

In 1908 Charles de Clifford came to Orepuki and took over the licence of the Masonic Hotel. He was only 18 years old when he managed his father's hotel at Seacliff in Otago. In 1912 he shifted to Riverton where he became established in the Railway Hotel. After a spell in Timaru he returned to Riverton and the Wallace County Hotel in Palmerston Street where he died in 1938 aged 64 years.

Fifty-one Dry Years!

In 1862 Gore was but a mere 6½ acres of practically empty ground. You could have bought the entire area for about £300 ($600). The long ford over the Mataura River can be claimed to be the principal reason for the existence of Gore. It is not known for sure who discovered the ford or who named it. Some think it could have been Alex McNab who ran sheep on both sides of the river. W. H. S. Roberts wrote "The ford was called 'long' because it went such a distance down stream from a shingle beach on the east to the landing on the west bank."

This drawing is of MacGibbon's Hotel at the long ford in the 1860s. Today the Longford Tavern trades in Hamilton Street, East Gore. MacGibbon and Sons also traded as merchants in East Gore in 1878 along with Mulvey's Hotel and Costello's Hotel . . .

In June 1903 prohibition was carried in the Mataura Electorate and not restored until 13 November 1954. Fifty-one dry years meant that the original hotels fell into disrepair and were demolished or were converted for other uses. Unlike rural Otago, rural Southland and Dunedin City there are no original hotels still trading so I have had to rely on historical records to include the township of Gore – named in 1862 after the then Governor Gore-Brown.

The Railway Hotel at Mandeville

Near the turn of the 19th century, James Roche was mine host of this hotel and his advertisement in the *Mills and Dick Business Directory* of the time stated that "Within minutes you can walk to and be fishing on three of Southland's best rivers – the Waimea, the Otemete and the Mataura." Also mentioned was the important fact that there was good paddock accommodation for your horse. Such were the tourist drawcards in our pioneering days. In 1936, E. B. Ostlund was the proprietor and he was advertising the very same fishing delights. The only difference was that "motorists were especially catered for . . ."

This is no longer a pub but the site of one of the province's finest restaurants, nestled close to the famed Mandeville Aero Museum and Aerodrome. In 1953 I travelled down from Dunedin to work for a week or two in Gore and quickly found that I had to travel 11 miles to Mandeville for a convivial drink and conversation – what a busy place that was on a Friday night!

When I eventually went back to see if there was any part of the old pub that I could recognise this was the result. Not much I agree, but it certainly brought back memories of a crowded bar and equally crowded car park.

Harliwich's Carrington Hotel

CHARLES CREBA,
GENERAL
Blacksmith & Horseshoer.
WAIKAIA
Mining and Agricultural Implements Made and Repaired.
CHOW YOKE,
General Merchant,
WAIKAIA.
Select and Varied Stocks of every District Requirement.

Gore is not the ideal town in which to record hotels, past or present. Before the town went dry in 1903 there were a number of elegant hotels serving the travellers and the drinkers, among them being the Southland, Railway Commercial, Holland's Gore Hotel, the Provincial, Club, Criterion and this one in Ashton Street. Sadly, there is very little evidence of these once-grand monuments to the god Bacchus still standing in Gore's business district but, during the 51 years, it's not surprising that these buildings would virtually disappear. Nowadays the hotels in Gore are rather bland affairs so I have delved back into history. I'm sure you will forgive me. This hotel was built of red brick, complete with the much-used Victorian window embellishments as used by architects such as Burwell, Sharp and Brodrick who were responsible for many of the classic buildings in Southland.

The Green Roofs of Wallacetown

In 1891 Wallacetown's blacksmith was Mrs H. Mann. Now, that's 115 years ago and even today that would probably raise a few eyebrows. J. Grieve and Co. were the storekeepers, the saddler was Colin Brown, the hotel keeper was H. H. Powell and the clergyman's position was vacant!

At Wallacetown Junction – obviously a separate settlement – there was a bacon factory run by W. Quinn and the freezing works were managed by George Mackley. The Junction Hotel licensee was D. O'Keefe. The only proprietors of this hotel that I knew personally were Roberta and Lou Purse. Roberta was an enthusiastic landscape artist whom I met first when she exhibited at the Anderson Park Art Gallery in 1962 when she and Lou were the licensees of the Green Roofs as it was popularly known. This wooden building has been very well maintained over the years and it sits snugly in a hollow beside the Riverton-Invercargill highway. Wallacetown is now a very attractive village with a roadside reserve being developed on the eastern side along with new tree and flower plantings the length of the road through the township.

Lorneville Junction Hotel

This pub is now known as the White House just down the road from the Green Roofs at Wallacetown.

When Invercargill was a dry area, this pub was the happy hunting ground for those folk with a motor car and room enough for a few kegs of ale and perhaps a bottle or two of spirits which was then delivered to a thirsty consumer in the city. There are many apocryphal stories of local taxi drivers "running the cutter" with booze hidden in the spare wheel cover which, in the early days of motoring, was situated forward of the front doors. This was in the days when cars had running boards and huge front mudguards.

I've heard it said that some taxi drivers made more, running booze from this pub, than they did from collecting fares! This may be only half true but it's a good story, isn't it?

Three well-known and respected publicans were Ivan West, Jim Muir and W. E. Hazlett. Hazlett ruled in the days when 45 barmen served huge crowds from behind the longest bar in New Zealand. I spoke to Jim Muir recently who reminded me of the introduction of the half crown (25c) jug and his wife's tasty lunches which went down well on sale days when the Lorneville Sale Yards were buzzing with stock agents, truck drivers, farmers and sundry onlookers. In later years the Rafter's Bar was one of the most popular venues with the iconic "Vision" rock band entertaining a packed house every week for years. How things have changed since those dry days in Invercargill.

126

Colac Bay Tavern

Colac is apparently a phonetic rendition of Korako, who was a local chief, but I find the connection a bit tenuous. The area has ancient Maori links such as the local Maori argillite carvings that are carbon dated to about 1200 AD. It is believed that it was used to make cutting tools. The first settlement was begun in 1850 but with the arrival of the railway in 1881 the times were changing. Timber from our wonderful native bush was milled in the district and shipped from the Pine Company wharf and by rail. In those days there were three sawmilling companies at Colac. In 1882 James A. Fish completed his "Bayview House" and a bottle licence was granted. At the same time Edward Hopgood applied for a certificate to authorise the issue of a publican's licence. This was the beginning of the Railway Hotel.

Edward Hopgood moved away from his Colac interests in about 1883 but his wife Susan remained and became involved in several successful business ventures such as a grocery business and the local post office. A new manager for the hotel was installed in about 1886 by the name of Patrick Molloy but his tenure was short-lived as he was prone to bouts of delerium tremens due to the vast amounts of liquor he consumed. While this unfortunate fellow was at the Railway Hotel in Riverton the local doctor refused to admit him to the hospital when he was in the grip of the demon drink and he died that very night aged 50.

Other publicans down through the years have been Charles and William Hopgood, Alphonso Manley, Thomas Edgerton, Alan Weeds, Joseph Hilderbrand and Pat McClinchy to name just a few. Almost every bar in Southland and Otago that I visited during the compiling of this book has some unique feature such as a poem, a cartoon or historic photographs.

Dusty's Bar at Colac has a game of skill and patience called "The Bull Ring". On one of the walls, just above eye level, is a large hook. About two metres away from the wall, suspended from the ceiling is a stout cord on which is attached a metal bull ring. The aim of the game is to gently swing the ring on the string so that it lands neatly on the hook on the wall. Sounds easy? Well, you have to be joking! It can be the most infuriatingly difficult task you have ever attempted. A former licensee, Kevin Mulqueen, holds the record of 59 consecutive rings. Next time you are in Dusty's Bar at Colac Bay, have a yarn to Dusty and Carole and try your luck at "The Bull Ring".

The Pavilion

In the early 1880s there was an orphanage on this site. The *Western Star* reported in 1883 that there were only five children in residence and that it may soon be empty. Nothing more has been recorded. In behind this building there once was a boarding house run by Mr and Mrs Tatar Shirley. In 1937 the local Railway Hotel was burnt to the ground and the present Colac Bay Tavern was built by the Invercargill cordial manufacturer A. B. Moffett and Co. Meanwhile another modern concept was being planned by Ulric Smith and his brother. A beach pavilion! Ulric approached his father John Willie Smith, founder of the iconic Southland Department Store – H. & J. Smith Ltd – for assistance in this far-sighted project and they were given the go ahead. Blue and Lindsay Contractors were engaged to construct the building which was up and running just prior to World War II. The first proprietors were Mr and Mrs Len Harrington and two local girls, Eri McKay and Lucy Cross, were employed as waitresses, dressed in green smocks and orange aprons.

The present proprietor, Julie Guise, has retained the 1930s look complete with the original changing sheds. One can only imagine bathers in their neck-to-knee costumes emerging from the cubicles to take the few steps across the road to the surf. Sitting in the bar of the pavilion, you are virtually on the beach.

The Celtic at Browns

This settlement was once known as "The Gap" because of its geographical position among a range of Limestone Hills. In 1897 McFarlane Brown became the district's first hotelier and from then on the village became known as Browns.

In 1896 Charles Hinde opened the first post and telegraph office in the local store. Forty-five years ago Browns was a real hub of industry considering its rural setting. There was a sawmill, a limeworks, claytile and brickworks all using the local deposits and the rail line from Winton to Hedgehope was in full use until its closure in 1966.

The hotel licence survived and today Browns has a volunteer fire brigade, a transport company and a primary school which opened in 1905 and has managed to survive the ravages of school closures. Browns is still known as the home of that wonderful lime which can lay claim to have been responsible for most of Southland's lush pastures.

But towering above that claim to fame is the legendary Browns Athletic Society's Annual Meeting, which in 1998 celebrated its centenary. Justine Harvey and Dave Twaddle are now your hosts at the Celtic at Browns. Drop in and try the food.

The Club at Bluff

This F. W. Burwell designed building was a busy place in 1891 when Andrew Scott was mine host. He advertised that he had hot, cold and shower baths, an excellent billiard table and good stabling. In 1870 Hannah Ward converted her boarding house into an hotel which she called the Club. Hannah was the mother of Joseph Ward who later became Prime Minister of New Zealand and later still, Sir Joseph.

Three years earlier the Bluff-to-Invercargill railway was opened which meant that Campbelltown (later re-named Bluff) became a very busy port town. The young Joseph Ward and his wife once bought 25 of the 66 prime waterfront surveyed sections, showing a certain business acumen, even at an early age. He went on to work for the post office, the new railway and his own store before becoming a borough councillor in 1878.

In 1892 he was elected to the House of Representatives. In that same year he set up the Ocean Beach Freezing Company. He later moved to Invercargill, became Prime Minister and was later honoured with a knighthood and is known as "Bluff's most famous son". In 1983 Murray and Dianne Flynn became the hosts of this historic hotel.

The Bayview at Bluff

Joseph Metzger built and operated this hotel until 1908 when he leased it out. Since then at least two dozen proprietors have come and gone. Originally it had four guest bedrooms along with a workshop and stables.

Bluff can claim to be perhaps the oldest settlement in New Zealand with James Spencer stepping ashore in 1824, thirteen years before Riverton was declared a borough. Spencer was born in 1790 and saw action in the Battle of Waterloo. He became a store and tavern-keeper and, in a roundabout way, was responsible for the first Bluff shipwreck. It seems that the crew of the ironically-named *Success* were in Spencer's tavern refreshing themselves when their ship fouled its anchor and eventually sank. There was never a dull moment in those hurly-burly days in Campbelltown.

The Railway at Nightcaps

Nightcaps – what a strange name for a town! I have never heard of or read a definitive explanation of why it was named thus. One anecdote suggests that the early settlers saw a resemblance to a silhouette formed by the hills behind the town or perhaps the fact that these same hills are regularly capped with snow or mist. However the original reason for the settlement was that in the 1860s a coalfield of considerable size was first noticed by a boundary rider from Birchwood Station. In 1880 the Nightcaps Coal Co. was established and the Ohai-Nightcaps region became the province's fuel centre and still is to this day.

The original Railway Hotel was a wooden structure, established in 1887. Like so many of the early hotels built of wood, it burned down in the 1950s and was rebuilt in an almost art deco design. Hotels of a smilar style can be seen at Benmore and Garston – perhaps they had the same builder.

In 1934 the publican was Frank Boyle, a name well known in Southland hotel circles.

In 1891 there was a library, E. Hunt was the local baker and A. Miller and J. Quested were the butchers. The hotel was run by B. J. Kelleher who also ran the Public Hall. The saddler was J. Clapp, Miss Jaggers was the local schoolmistress and the three general stores were run by G. Groves, A. Miller and J. Clapp and incidentally this hotel is situated at No. 1 Clapp Street.

John and Annette Blackler are the present licensees who took command of the local thirsts on 18 November 1996.

Holland's Gore Hotel

From 1877 to 1882 it was known as East Gore, then from 1882 it was Gordon — and lo and behold – in 1890 they began to call it East Gore again, as it has remained thus to this day. A little confusing you will agree. This rather substantial wooden building – J. Holland's Gore Hotel – was probably part of the village centre in 1891. Earlier in 1883 there were two hotels, The Provincial run by Mrs T. Mulvey and Monaghans Commercial. I wonder if Greg. Mulvey, the general manager of the Invercargill Licensing Trust is a distant relative of Mrs Mulvey? Perhaps the licensed trade is in the blood.

It's interesting to note that in the 1890 the Gore district had no less than six accoucheurs. For those of you like myself who, until recently had no idea what an accoucheur was, the answer is "midwife". No doubt Mesdames Pollock, How, Currie, Greig, De Terte and Hutchinson were very busy people in the pre-pill big family era.

When next you are in the area take note of the street names that surveyor W. V. Hall gave to East Gore. Herries Beatty in his 1962 *History of Gore and District* wrote "apparently no one has worked out why he chose a mixture of English and Canadian names".

The South Seas, Stewart Island

This hotel is listed as a "country style" establishment. How could it be anything else in this remote part of New Zealand? This first time I set foot on this little bit of heaven was in the '60s and I can well remember being absolutely enchanted with the beauty, the solitude and the fact that I was only 30k from Bluff. It felt like there was nowhere else in the world. My first meal in the tiny dining room of the South Seas was truly memorable. The blue cod was only hours out of the pristine waters that surround Rakiura (Glowing Sky) and after eating fish that fresh you will never want it any other way. Captain Cook sailed around parts of the island in 1770 but mistook it for a peninsula attached to the mainland and called it South Cape. Captain William Stewart charted this island in 1809 and Rakiura became Stewart Island.

On 19 January 1978 I flew to the island with Murray Donald in an old Grumman Widgeon ZKBGQ. It was the last flight of this reliable old plane which, on landing in the bay, ran up onto the beach, almost to the road which separated the sand from the pub. Where else in New Zealand can you literally fly to an hotel?

Over the years I have travelled to Rakiura on the m.v. *Wairua,* the new modern ferry, amphibian aircraft, *Britten Norman Islander,* and in the open cockpit of a Tiger Moth. However your travel to this haven, the food and the beer always tastes better than on the mainland.

Waikiwi Bush Hotel

The Waikiwi Bush Hotel was one of the earliest licensed premises in the district. In the days when this tiny pub was operating it was far enough away from the fledgling town of Invercargill that if you didn't have a horse or you weren't able to walk, you could catch the train which ran from Invercargill and back at regular intervals from 7.30 am till 8.30 in the evening. In 1891 the licensee was Thomas A. Stephens who also kept the local store and post office. There were two nurserymen, three brickmakers and the butcher was James Metzger – I wonder if the street in the city was named after him.

The Governor Grey

This was once a well-known landmark in the city of Invercargill – the former Governor Grey Hotel in Dee Street. Built in 1883, the proprietor was Wyld Stark, father of the legendary "Starkie" of World War I. He was the soldier who would, they say, have been awarded the Victoria Cross had he not been in so much trouble with the military authorities. Like his contemporary Southlander Dick Travis, V.C. Starkie was known to go off on one-man forays into no man's land during the awfulness of the war in France, kill a few Germans and then return to his trench. It was said that this completely demoralised the enemy.

Travis was a little different in that he collected information on his trips into the unknown but was nonetheless regarded as meritorious. "Starkie" returned to New Zealand and saw out his days in sad, squalid conditions in Auckland. At the time Wyld Stark was dispensing fine ale and hospitality, Invercargill had no less than 33 hotels then, in 1906, the prohibitioners won the slimmest of polls and everyone of the town's hotels closed until 1944 – a long dry spell! But apparently it had little or no effect on the excessive drinking the town had become renowned for.

When I drew this old building, a real local character had just opened a coffee bar. His name was Don McElhinney, a labour stalwart who would argue politics till the cows came home. Don never lost his faith in his party, even when it took a turn to the right and National's Muldoon was taking a left turn. What interesting days they were for the average voter but bewildering for those who remained steeped in the dogma of Micky Savage.

"The Ugliest Tavern Ever"

Soon after Invercargill became "wet" in 1944, plans were being made to erect temporary bars around the city. In 1860 the Clarendon Hotel stood on this site – the corner of Esk and Kelvin Streets. This was one of a few kitset buildings which were built under the supervision of the Public Works Dept using ex-Defence Dept Buildings left over from the war.

I can well remember the brown linoleum on the floor and the large ashtrays at your feet as you breasted the bar. In earlier times they would be called spittoons. And do you remember the rail at the base of the bar that served as a foot rest? The refinements in those bars were almost too many to mention! I think there were a couple of pot belly stoves strategically placed in that rectangle of pleasure and recreation. But no stools or seats. That was considered rather "effete" among the beer drinkers of the '40s and '50s.

Another unique feature of these drinking establishments were the rows of bicycle stands outside. On Saturday afternoon between 5 pm and 6 pm there wasn't a space to be had and believe it or not there were very few thefts despite the fact that there wasn't a fancy bike lock to be seen.

Soon after this bar was finished a writer to the editor of *The Southland Times* asked, "Who on earth at City Hall approved the plans for this hideous erection?" However it served its purpose until 26 January 1965 – the walls and ceiling, sticky and yellow with nicotine and the floor sodden with the gallons of beer that had seeped through the cracks in the lino. There was a similar tavern in Clyde Street. Opened in 1944 and rebuilt in brick in 1958, it closed in 1991 ending the era of unattractive taverns.

A Grand Old Lady

In 1953 there was a Royal tour of New Zealand being planned and it included Invercargill . . . In those days a tour by the Royal Family was a huge occasion and no end of meticulous planning (sometimes taken to ridiculous extremes) was occupying the minds of members of the relatively new Invercargill Licensing Trust. You see, the young Queen Elizabeth II and her Royal party were to be housed in our finest hotel for two nights – the last two nights of the tour before embarking on the s.s. *Gothic* from Bluff in January 1965. Her Majesty made her final broadcast to the nation from the lounge of this hotel, a lounge I was very familiar with in my capacity of musician. For four years I worked with a trio in the large, elegant lounge, perhaps the best gig this band ever had. George Mertz was the manager at the time and many a young man was turned away because he wasn't wearing a tie. On one occasion he went upstairs and got one of his own and presented it to the hapless male!

My, how things have changed. The Grand is no longer licensed but is a boarding establishment for students at the Southern Institute of Technology. A very comfortable place to live and right in the middle of town too!

The Cecil

This hotel on the corner of Tay and Kelvin Streets was originally the Milford. I used to take the odd tincture there from time to time. When you reached the head of the stairs you walked into a lounge area complete with piano and sometimes a pianist. When the new Kelvin was opened it was decided that the Cecil in Kelvin Street and Deschlers in Esk street would be surplus to requirements. This was in 1974 and I believe the closure was hastened when, at the end of the year, a series of fights broke out on a Friday night and to compound it all the "biffo" was witnessed by none other than the chairman of the Licensing Trust, Ollie Henderson, who immediately decreed that the bar must close. This brought to an end a colourful era in our hotel history.

But there was more to come from within these historic walls. In 1980 a group of local businessmen bought the building and established the province's first private radio station – Foveaux Radio. In 1984 I was approached to initiate the first talk radio show. When I asked why I was selected I was told, "you have a big mouth with an ego to match!"

I wasn't exactly flattered but the show lasted 16 years without intruding on my work of drawing and painting pictures. I was fortunate to have had the opportunity of interviewing and getting to know hundreds of characters that I otherwise would not have met and enjoyed. The old Cecil will always have a special place in my heart.

Edwardian and Baroque Revival

This is another in the long line of railway hotels in New Zealand. It was built in 1896 right opposite the main entrance of the new wooden railway station. The station has been rebuilt in a modern style and was a busy place until railway, as a means of transporting people became obsolete. They blame it on the motor car but I can't remember trains killing as many people as cars do in this so called enlightened age.

This is one of Invercargill's finest architectural gems, fully restored and operational. In 1864 on the site of this beautiful building, there stood an iron store operated by Burgoyne and Sons. In 1876 the store was replaced by Smith's Railway Hotel, then in 1896 the present hotel was built. The architect was C. J. Brodrick and the first owner was Mr I. W. Raymond. In this drawing I've shown a section of the very ornate parapet topped by a triangular pediment. The octagonal tower with cupola and finial stands above the parapet and is a truly beautiful section of this classic building. We must be truly thankful that this building has been spared the demolisher's hammer and ball. Sadly there has been too much real estate vandalism in years past but I think it is slowing as we realise that our history was disappearing before our eyes.

Princess Hotel

In 1883 Mrs J. Bridge ran this small hotel and I can well remember in 1956 when I arrived in Invercargill it was still standing – well just – perhaps leaning would be a better word. It had acquired a second storey and I often peered through a half-open door and wondered what it had been like in its heyday . . .

If my memory serves me right it was in the '60s that an accountant by the name of Maurice Campbell took it unto himself to demolish this old pub and develop the second only shopping arcade in the City of Invercargill – Courtville Place. This was a real novelty as this was a concept we were quite unfamiliar with. However it still serves a purpose and whenever I'm in this vicinity I tend to remember that relic that once stood proudly among eight other hotels in the long wide street called Dee. I've seen quite bewildering change during the 50 years I've spent in this part of the world and I was reminded of this recently as I read some of John A. Lees memories and I quote, "we marvel at the unrest in society because we refuse to realise that more significant changes in the circumstances of life have occurred in 100 years than in the previous 2,000" . . . how true . . .

The Royal Standard of England

I couldn't resist the temptation to include this drawing I made in England in 1984. It's the oldest I've ever visited and it is said to have been in existence, in one form or another, since 1084. On a fine Sunday afternoon, we drove about 30 miles north of London and happened upon this gem at Beaconsfield.

King Charles II sheltered here during his flight to France in 1651 after having the sauce kicked out of him at the Battle of Worcester (it's still called hot sauce, isn't it!)

I sat in the Charles Room and looked aloft to the roof where the King was hidden. At this time it was called Ye Ship but after the reformation Charles honoured his hiding place by bestowing upon it the imposing title of The Royal Standard of England. It leans in all directions these days but that adds to the charm of this monument to days gone by. But the reason for including my drawing of this pub is because of the wonderful restoration and upkeep of this and many other buildings in England. A lot of them were built originally of wattle and daub (mud) and timbers of great age and maturity – and they have survived. Parts of this building have been restored with timbers and bricks from an 800-year-old structure but some of the original mud walls, built in the 13th century, still stand.

Many of the oldest pubs I have depicted in Central Otago that were built of either sun-dried brick, stone or wattle and daub have withstood the ravages of the harsh, dry climate for up to 145 years, so let's hope they are treated with respect for another century or two.